R01172 70340

D0891975

How To Avoid

The **10** Biggest

Homebuying
Traps

A.M. WATKINS

PATRICK HOGAN

6th Edition

Real Estate
Education Company
a division of Dearborn Financial Publishing, Inc.

This publication is designed to provide accurate and authoritative information in regard to the subject matter covered. It is sold with the understanding that the publisher is not engaged in rendering legal, accounting or other professional service. If legal advice or other expert assistance is required, the services of a competent professional person should be sought.

Acquisitions Editor: Christine E. Litavsky
Managing Editor: Jack Kiburz
Interior Design: Lucy Jenkins
Cover Design: S. Laird Jenkins Corporation

©1968, 1972, 1977, 1984, 1988, 1996 by A. M. Watkins

Published by Real Estate Education Company®,
a division of Dearborn Financial Publishing, Inc.®

Printed in the United States of America

96 97 98 10 9 8 7 6 5 4 3 2 1

Library of Congress Cataloging-in-Publication Data

Watkins, A. M. (Arthur Martin), 1924—
   How to avoid the 10 biggest homebuying traps / by A. M.
Watkins and Patrick Hogan.—6th ed.
     p. cm.
   Includes index.
   ISBN 0-7931-1338-5 (pbk.)
   1. House buying. I. Hogan, Patrick. II. Title.
TH4817.5.W37   1996   95-26828
643'.12—dc20   CIP

Contents

Preface

"Why is it that whenever somebody buys a house they need a new roof within a year?"

So asked one wry friend of ours at a time when many of us were buying our first houses. You can count on discovering something new about the house you just purchased in the first month after you move in. We wrote this book to help you avoid bad surprises.

When you study customer satisfaction surveys or complaints and lawsuits in the real estate industry, you'll see the same problems coming up again and again. We did, and that's what gave us the idea to choose the ten biggest home-buying traps that make up this book. We've considered the principles of quality design, materials and construction in houses. We also offer advice in handling the legal and financial parts of the bargain in a sound, businesslike manner.

If you keep your eyes on the traps, you'll also know quality when you see it. This book is all about making the best decisions when buying a home. That means understanding how to work with the real estate agent and knowing if she works for you or the seller. It means recognizing what's good design inside and out in a house. And it means making money-saving mortgage choices.

Should you buy a new house or a used house? If you're like most people, your preference is based on preconceptions: "They don't build them like they used to," or, "With a new house we won't have to worry about any maintenance because it's brand new." We have provided eye-opening advice for either choice. You may think that buying a top-of-the-line new home will save you from trouble, but not if you're dealing with a vanishing builder. We'll tip you off on the warning signs. If you're buying a used house, we'll help you steer clear of the lemon. We describe the most common house ailments, including environmental problems like radon, lead and asbestos.

When you're avoiding traps you'll be saving money. You'll negotiate the best deal. Amidst the wide variety of mortgage products, you'll choose wisely the best for your financial situation. You'll stay away from the energy guzzling home that would be a hole in your wallet. And you won't pay for gimmicks that turn out to be more trouble than they're worth.

This is the book that we wish we had when we bought our first houses.

We hope it offers you useful ideas and advice, especially how to avoid the major traps that have long hurt home buyers. Good luck.

■ ══ CHAPTER 1 ══ ■

The High-Priced House

Nobody wants to lose money by paying more for a house than it is worth, even though it happens, alas, time after time. And everybody realizes they can profit substantially by knowing how to avoid the high-priced house. Yet, paying too much for a house is a frequent trap because so many houses are overpriced.

We once saw a four-bedroom house that was offered for sale at $435,000. What a surprise. It simply wasn't worth that much money. Sure enough, the house didn't sell until a year and a half later and only after the owner dropped the price to $295,000. At the same time, another house right down the street was put on the market for $385,000. It was similar in size and style and sold in three weeks! The house sold because it was in far better condition throughout. The first house had been neglected for years and showed it. It was overpriced, and homebuyers instinctively knew it.

Overpricing a house is one of the most common mistakes made by sellers. Many owner-sellers have wildly inflated ideas of the value of their own little, or not so little, homesteads. Or they have dreams of glory about making a killing. But lightning doesn't strike, and the houses go unsold for eons of time, it seems. Sellers can pay an expensive price for this type of miscalculation.

The high-priced house becomes a white elephant. Because it stands there lonely and apparently unwanted, a stigma grows attached to it, like moss on a log. Finally, the house has to be marked down to be sold, like surplus merchandise in a bargain basement.

■ KNOW YOUR MARKET

The best way to defend yourself against paying too much for a house is to understand the state of the market when you are buying. House prices in the United States grew at record rates in the 1980s. It seemed as if house prices could only go up. The market was booming. Houses were selling quickly, often in competitive situations with multiple bidders. Buyers felt a sense of urgency. It seemed as if the longer you waited, the more you would end up paying. Many buyers, determined to nail down their dream home, knowingly paid too much. They were confident that rapid appreciation would make up the difference in no time. But you can't take growth for granted. The 1980s housing boom skidded to a halt (not long after the stock market crash in 1987). Many new homeowners in southern California also learned the hard way after defense industry cuts led to high unemployment, and the value of many homes dropped below their purchase price.

In short, real estate goes through up and down market cycles as do other industries, moving from growth to maturity and topping out, followed by a period of decline until hitting bottom and growing once again. The law of supply and demand is ever present. Be an astute buyer and understand the market's cycles. Watch economic indicators. In a period of growth, business is expanding, unemployment is low, building is active, and houses sell quickly. In a market decline, the newspapers are filled with grim news of layoffs and foreclosures. New building may continue, but real estate is harder to sell. It's more difficult to get financing

And most important, sellers are more likely to make price concessions and even offer generous terms such as seller financing. As the cycle bottoms out, building catches its breath and demand once again begins to grow and catch up with supply.

A special economic indicator to watch is interest rates. In the early 1980s, prices for many houses fell because of high mortgage interest rates. When interest rates decline, house sales climb and prices firm up. House prices can also be affected by the local economy. In Seattle, Washington, for example, house prices can vary according to the fortunes of the Boeing Corporation, Seattle's largest employer. Mass layoffs at Boeing can cast a pall over the area. Similarly, problems in the oil industry in the 1980s sent Houston's real estate market into a nose dive from which it took years to recover. No matter where you live, staying abreast of the housing market, locally and nationally, could give you insight into buying a house that could pay off for you in big money savings.

If you plan to buy a home locally, drive around with your eyes open. Are there many For Sale signs? How quickly are homes moving? REALTORS® have access to the Multiple Listing Service (MLS) that keeps records on all homes on the market, including selling prices of recent sales. If you are working with a REALTOR®, you should be able to obtain printouts of recent sales within specific areas. Selling prices are often reported in local newspapers, though those sales may be a few months old.

Such information is increasingly available on-line through computer databases. One such service is Home Sales Line, an interactive computer system that can be accessed through an 800 number by phone and fax in a number of states to search for price information. Ask around and see your newspaper's real estate section to learn about similar services in your area.

■ HOW APPRAISERS DETERMINE MARKET VALUE

When you shop for a house, you learn about current house values by keeping your eyes open and asking questions. Study the market and compare prices, check new prices, and find out what houses sold for recently. In time, you will acquire a sense for the values of houses. Seeing a house, you will quickly have a good idea of its worth. You can also get a good idea of house values from real estate agents. They will give you the asking price of every house for sale they show you.

In most cases, a professional appraiser will evaluate the house. Usually your lender will order an appraisal (at your expense) before your mortgage can be approved. The appraiser collects data about the property, the market, the location, zoning regulations or any other factors that influence the value of the house. An appraiser takes into consideration such factors as the cost to rebuild a comparable house on the same site, less depreciation, the recent sales of houses and land in the same neighborhood, and adds a good dose of professional judgment based on experience.

An appraisal can cost roughly $200 to $400, depending on where you live. It may or may not make sense to get an appraisal before bidding on a house, but it is an option. When you zero in on a house that you want to buy but are unsure of how much it's really worth, getting an appraisal can resolve your doubts and give you an accurate basis for the price you pay. But use a certified appraiser. Look for someone who is a designated member of a professional appraisal association, such as the Appraisal Institute, the American Society of Appraisers, the National Association of Master Appraisers or the National Association of Independent Fee Appraisers. Appraisers are listed in the Yellow Pages. A good idea, especially if you know where you'll be getting your mortgage, is to ask the lender for a recommendation. Ask also if you can use the appraisal report for your mortgage approval, and hence save several hundred dollars.

FIGURE 1.1 ■

A fine old house like this eighteenth-century colonial house can be worth virtually any price (in satisfaction as well as in money). Note the excellent proportion and symmetry of its design. It is the Julius Deming House, Litchfield, Connecticut, built in 1790, a classic example of Federal architecture. (*Photo: Wayne Andrews*)

■ THE IMPORTANCE OF LOCATION

Because location exerts a powerful influence on the value of houses, it rates a few more words. Many of us have seen houses that command premium prices because they're on a lovely lake frontage or in a highly desirable "name" area. There's Grosse Pointe outside of Detroit, Shaker Heights outside of Cleveland, River Oaks in Houston. A virtually identical house a few miles away in a so-so location will sell for considerably less. The location makes the difference.

The reverse situation is the house that may be an excellent buy except—and here's when to beware—it is located in a neighborhood that is quietly going downhill. You may not know it, but the old-timers are fleeing; commercial development is slated to begin soon. All the old houses are eroding away in value simply because of a developing change for the worse. There may be few visible signs of the downhill slide to the inexperienced eye, but it could be going on nevertheless. This puts special emphasis on checking the value of a house in an area that's unfamiliar to you.

On the other hand, some houses can represent quite a bargain buy in an area or neighborhood that in the opposite way was formerly considered undesirable but is slowly and inexorably on the upgrade. It may be an area benefiting from renewal or simply one that has been out of fashion but is picking itself up by its bootstraps. Some classic examples are found in old sections of large cities that have been coming back in recent years. Latch on to a good house in such a place before the neighborhood improvement becomes generally known, and often you can get yourself quite a buy.

It's also important to check on the local zoning rules, assuming you don't want to see those lovely woods across the street invaded by bulldozers someday to make way for a new shopping center or chemical factory. Your best protection is an area that is strictly zoned chiefly for residential use, permitting little or no other kind of development. If there are commercial and industrial zones nearby, watch out.

You should, in fact, be particularly wary of buying a house near any sizable piece of vacant, undeveloped land. Unless there are firm plans for the development of that land, who knows what will happen to it? If it is later developed for commercial use or for cheap housing, it could sharply downgrade the value of the rest of the area around, including your house.

Among other things, check on how zealously the local politicians guard the zoning regulations. If they have a past record of allowing little or no down-zoning of residential property (to allow the cheapest house or other construction), that's fine. But if they're fast and loose with the zoning rules, they're likely to be fast and loose with what they allow to be built near the house you buy.

■ BUYING A FOR SALE BY OWNER (FSBO)

For Sale by Owner—the real estate industry calls them fizzbos. About one in ten buyers buys a house directly from a seller, with no real estate agents involved. This number might strike you as low. After all, when sellers use an agent they pay a commission. If the commission can be avoided, there's more room for both buyer and seller to come out ahead. However, because there are pitfalls in dealing directly with the seller, many buyers prefer to use agents.

Watch out when you are looking at a FSBO, because so many owners have an exaggerated sense of what their homes are worth. When the market is hot, owners are more likely to sell without an agent, and they feel entitled to their high asking price. Oftentimes a seller knows very little about house prices in the area, though this is essential information that every good agent knows. In an active market, real estate becomes a hot topic of conversation in the community. The only market analysis going on may be sellers hearing how much the Joneses got for a house that, of course, isn't nearly as nice as their property. Whereas the agent focuses on making a sale, the owner-seller may latch on to the price as a point of pride.

It also can be difficult to negotiate directly with owners. A buyer can often be shy about confronting an owner with drawbacks to the house. On the other hand, with an agent, a buyer can openly question price and comment on the owner's decor and the cost to redecorate. Similarly, sellers can be highly sensitive to criticisms that are typical in the bargaining process. One buyer took a look at a fizzbo house and was promptly ready to start negotiating. First she indicated to the owners some areas of wear on the roof and suggested that she thought work was needed. She was seriously interested in making a bid. This was just her opener to starting talks. For whatever reason, the owners reacted by taking the home off the market until the roof repairs could be made. Maybe the owners were embarrassed by this shortcoming. Maybe deep down they didn't want to sell. The situation was strange, because it was the second time the sellers had pulled the home from the market. The eager buyer was left hanging; wondering why. Never underestimate the pride that sellers have in their houses. An agent would take this comment from the prospective buyer for what it was and could diplomatically explain to the owners the rationale for a low bid.

Some FSBO sellers deliberately price high, trying to get top dollar. They're from the P. T. Barnum school, believing that a sucker is born every minute. The trouble is that nobody wants to be that sucker. And when reasonable people come in with a reasonable offer, the owner may nevertheless be insulted and refuse to counter. You can imagine the situation when the buyer comes in with a mirrored strategy of making a low-ball offer to see if a seller might accept it.

So while it seems like FSBOs should be a great opportunity to save money on a purchase, they rarely work out that way. Real estate agents perform a screening function. Good agents won't take a listing unless the owner is truly motivated to sell and is asking a reasonable price, or is at least within negotiating range of reasonable. If you see an overpriced FSBO that you really like but anticipate problems in the negotiating, it might be an appropriate time to hire your own appraiser. You can use the appraisal report in your negotiations as a rationale for your offer and to insert objectivity in an exchange that might otherwise become emotionally charged.

■ THE NEW HOUSE

You may be able to save some money on a new house, depending on the builder you buy it from. You can buy from an investor/builder who buys one lot and builds a single house to sell. Or you can buy from a developer who sub-divides a track of land, builds a model house or two and takes orders to build houses in the subdivision. The following examples illustrate the difference.

A custom-house builder we know put a house he built up for sale at $125,000. The house did not sell for a while; the market was sluggish. He advertised more, but still no sale. A man came along and offered $115,000. The builder said no, but he would take $119,500, and the house was sold. The builder took what he could get rather than keep the house any longer.

That's the kind of new house—the already finished, speculatively built kind—that is most likely to be over-priced. It's therefore the new house that is most likely to be subject to bargaining, particularly if it has gone unsold for a while. It costs builders money every month to keep the house, so as time goes by they are increasingly open to any reasonable offer. Naturally, a builder is much tempted to overprice a new house with the hope of getting as much as possible at first. If it doesn't sell, he will ordinarily have to come down in price and take the best price he can get.

That's why a low first bid can save you money when you buy a speculative-builder house. You may be turned down, but you can come back with a higher offer. You may be amazed at how much you might save on the house.

New houses in new developments are much more likely to be firm in price. Generally you must pay the listed price, particularly for a new house that you order from the builder's model that he will build for you in the develop-ment. An exception is when a builder is closing out a tract of houses and has a few remaining houses, already finished, that he wants to unload. This is especially true if the houses have been standing unsold for a long time.

■ REAL ESTATE BROKERS AND THEIR AGENTS

A veteran homebuyer we know now holds a dim view of real estate brokers. He and his wife were being driven to a house by a broker who lauded to the skies its every characteristic. "It's an unbeatable buy," the broker said, reeling off one glowing feature after another. To our friend the house sounded increasingly familiar. He finally said, "It sounds like the Evans house. Another broker showed it to us."

The broker instantly turned the car around and without breaking verbal stride, proceeded to reel off all the things that were wrong with the house. He heard that it had termites and, among other things, that the furnace was in bad shape. The Evans house was definitely not for them, but he could take them to another, far better house!

Our friend decided to profit from the experience. To learn about possible flaws in a house for sale, he would casually mention the house to brokers other than the one who had shown him the house, stating frankly that he was interested in the house but had seen it through another broker. He says, "It's amazing how much you can learn about a house from a broker or agent who can't sell it to you."

There are about 1.2 million real estate licensees in the United States and, of course, not all are so shameless. In fact, real estate agents can help you in a lot of positive ways. The best agents usually will be among the 700,000 members of the National Association of REALTORS® (NAR). Though things have changed in recent years, many real estate agents have been part-timers—taxi drivers, housewives, carpenters, service station owners, people from all walks of life but not exactly dedicated to the real estate trade. No broker can use the designation REALTOR® without being a member of the association, and hence of their local board. REALTORS® subscribe to a professional code of ethics and are also afforded many educational opportunities. Though some non–REALTOR® agents may be top-notch, in general full-time REALTORS® tend to know the most about the local market. That's important because much of the service agents offer relates to the quality of their information and knowledge.

An agent should be an expert on a market. Agents have access to the MLS, a database of properties listed for sale, and can obtain information about properties throughout a wide area. The agent may also be a good source of information about the community—schools, churches, zoning regulations, development trends, municipal services and more. In addition, agents can also help you with all the hurdles along the way. They may advise you on your choices in the mortgage market and recommend lenders. Because the agent's commission depends on a successful closing of the sale, he or she will also help make sure that all the necessary paperwork is taken care of, including title insurance checks, home inspection reports and mortgage commitments.

Although our friend's distrust of agents may have been extreme, it does make sense to respect the fact that the agent is trying to sell you something and understand that they therefore have underlying motivations that may not be consistent with yours. You should be suspicious if agents seem to be steering you to certain houses that don't fit the criteria you've discussed, particularly if they are emphasizing houses listed by their own brokerage company. At the very least these agents are not doing a good job of listening; at worst they may be more interested in an attractive commission than in serving your needs. Also, despite our friend's success at uncovering possible flaws in a home, you should remember that very few agents are construction experts, so whatever an agent says, usually with great enthusiasm, about the structural condition of a house, it should be discounted heavily. "Look at all the insulation you'll get from those big thick stone walls," one may say, obviously totally ignorant of the fact that solid masonry has very little insulating value. Go to a construction expert or home inspector for such information, not to an agent. A real estate agent is expected to know no more about construction than a Wall Street broker is expected to know about computer circuits when he sells you stock in IBM. In fact, with all the lawsuits in our society, smart agents are very careful about making any representations about the condition of the home. In many states, seller disclosure laws requiring that specific problems be clearly stated in writing are taking agents off the hook.

In addition to construction, one service that perhaps you should not expect from your agent is negotiating, for the simple reason that your agent may be loyal to the seller, not you. Be sure you have a clear understanding right from the start of where your agent's fiduciary loyalty lies.

■ WHO DOES YOUR AGENT REPRESENT?

The real estate agent representing the homeowner is called the listing agent. In fact, all associate licensees of the listing brokerage company are officially listing agents. In the traditional real estate transaction, the agent who is working with the buyer, called the selling agent or cooperating agent, is a subagent of the seller and has a fiduciary duty to the seller. In other words, "your" agent owes complete loyalty to the seller and is charged with, among other things, obtaining the highest possible purchase price for the property.

Consumer surveys in the late 1980s showed that two-thirds of the people buying a home thought the agent with whom they worked was representing them. Pressures from consumer groups as well as some forces within the industry led to more and more states requiring that agents disclose to buyers in writing their agency relationship, that is, whom they represented in the transaction. Now nearly all states have some type of agency disclosure law. Seeing it all spelled out in black and white was an eye opener to many buyers and led to clamors for change in real estate transactions.

Nowadays buyers have more options. While buyer's agents have been around for some time, recent changes in NAR policy and the rules of the MLS system have been more accommodating toward buyer representation. There are two types of buyer agency—*exclusive buyer agency* and *disclosed dual agency* (also called *consensual dual agency*). In an exclusive relationship, the agent and the brokerage company represent buyers only; they do not take listings to sell homes. In disclosed dual agency, either the agent or perhaps just the brokerage handles listings. Therefore, the situation may arise that a home you want to purchase is listed by the same brokerage company with which your buyer's agent is associated. How the intricacies thereafter unfold varies by state or local laws, but what is critical is that there must be disclosure. Understandably, there is controversy within the industry over buyer agency in general, and opponents to dual agency will argue vehemently that it is a practical impossibility to represent in good faith both sides of a trans-action. If you choose to use buyer representation, you should be clear on whether the brokerage practices dual agency and, if so, how it is handled. Also, though buyer rep-resentation looks to be the wave of the future, it is still new in some parts of the country and is not always accepted. In time that will change, but it is possible that certain broker-ages will not want to deal with buyer's agents and, as a result, your field of choices may be smaller when using one.

When you choose to go with a buyer's agent, you will sign an agreement, just as a seller signs a listing agreement. The agreement will outline all the terms of your relation-ship, including the length of the contract and compensation arrangements. In many cases the agent will draw a commis-sion from the seller, or from the proceeds of the sale, just as a traditional subagent will. Compensation may also take the form of fee for service, hourly rate or retainer. If you are unsure about anything in the agreement, this might be a good time to involve a lawyer. You'll need legal advice eventually once it's time to make a purchase.

A few states have adopted a new option, the *facilitator*. In the facilitator relationship the agents involved in the transaction do not purport to represent either buyer or seller. Their role is to merely move the transaction forward and help both sides come to an agreement. In practice, this is not so far from how agents have been operating all along in the traditional real estate transaction. The forces of human nature tend to bend the strict requirements of agency law. After all, in working with a buyer over a period of weeks, maybe months, an agent could very well develop a sense of loyalty out of a personal bonding, whereas the seller is just a name on a listing sheet. In addition, the agent isn't paid any commission until there is a sale, and that might be strong enough motivation to go to bat for the buyer if it means bringing the two sides to agreement. Despite all the furor by advocates of buyer agency, the traditional transactions for the most part have not been such a big problem. The NAR Code of Ethics states that agents should treat both buyer and seller honestly and fairly, and good agents have always followed that dictum no matter whom they represent.

So now with all these choices, what's the best way to go? The Consumer Federation of America has contended that there should be opportunities to negotiate lower commission rates for homebuyers using dual agents or facilitators and that buyers should avoid the traditional subagent relationship altogether. But there are pros and cons either way, and you must make a judgment based on your situation and needs. For instance, if you are relocating to a new city, you may be inclined to choose a buyer's agent because you won't have much familiarity with the local market. On the other hand, if you consider yourself a good negotiator, you may prefer the freedom of the subagent scenario, where you are not tied down to any one agent. If you go for a buyer's agent, be careful in choosing your agent and don't commit to too long a time period, certainly not beyond 90 days, a typical period of a listing contract. Also, make sure that your agent is well informed on the specific neighborhoods you're searching. If you haven't focused on a specific area, that may be an argument against going with buyer agency. You don't want to be committed to an agent who is completely unfamiliar with the area where you're looking. Even worse, some agreements may obligate you to pay the buyer's agent a commission, regardless of whether or not that agent actually brings you to the home. A solution is to work with a brokerage that has offices all over town and offers the flexibility to switch to another office if you've changed your mind about neighborhoods.

Probably more important than the agency relationship is to work with a qualified, knowledgeable and professional agent. A buyer's agent who is a poor negotiator will not be of much help and, conversely, a subagent who provides you with lots of knowledge of the marketplace over time has empowered you to negotiate wisely. Your responsibility is to understand what the agency relationship is. If you are working with a subagent, or even a dual agent, be wary of disclosing any information regarding your financial resources, motivations or ceiling prices. You must recognize, however, that all real estate agents have a legitimate interest in confirming that you can afford the types of homes you're looking at, otherwise they would be wasting their time as well as yours. One way around this is to go to a lender first and get prequalified for a mortgage. Ask for a letter stating the approval that you can then show to the agent. Obviously the idea here is to request approval only for the level of mortgage you need to make a purchase in your desired price range. You're defeating the purpose if you prequalify for the maximum loan possible. Don't ever make statements to the subagent such as, "I want to offer $160,000, but I'm willing to go up to 170." The agent's legal obligation is to relay that information to the seller. Similarly, if you come across a house that you absolutely *must* have, you had best put on your poker face as you discuss it with the agent. Consider the subagent to be the eyes and ears of the seller.

■ BUYING STRATEGY

Now let's assume you have found a house you'd like to buy. You've checked on the value, the neighborhood and other such things (as detailed in later chapters). You're almost ready to make a bid. Before you do, try to determine how long the house has been on the market, a telling fact. The longer it has gone unsold, the more likely the owner will take a reduced price, and the lower your first offer can be.

To get a house at the lowest possible price, however, you must be prepared to lose it to a possible higher bidder. In any case, start low and don't worry too much. You can

FIGURE 1.2 ■

This Connecticut house offers an inviting entrance, fine outlooks from every floor level and, in short, a happy marriage with its site. A 4-star house. (*Architect: John Milnes Balcer, AIA, Katonah, N.Y. Photo: Tom Crane*)

always come back with a higher bid—and come back a third time even higher.

If you're averse to bargaining, use a buyer's agent or ask your lawyer do it for you. Or you can decide on the price you are willing to pay and offer that. There are certain people, astutely business-minded in other ways, who simply cannot face up to personal confrontation concerning money. They tend to pay whatever is asked for a house (or for anything else they buy) largely because of emotional makeup.

The asking price for a house is either the highest price the owner hopes to get or simply his starting point for negotiations, or both. A classified ad for the house may state, "Asking Price," and give a figure. Usually the owner will be receptive to any reasonable offer but also may say, "Make an offer."

Some sellers say their price is "firm." They imply they will settle for no less—or so they hope, often wishfully. If they don't get their price, however, many will face reality and come down. Others may take their houses off the market, and still others will indeed get huffy should someone make what they consider a ridiculously low offer. They feel their houses are worth every single dollar they ask. Such a house may or may not be worth the price, but it is up to you to decide. If it is worth the price, you must pay it or something close to it. More often than not, however, such people have delusions of grandeur. Their houses are sorely overpriced.

For houses priced up to about $150,000, more or less, the first bid may be at least 10 to 20 percent under the asking price. The higher the asking price, the more you may underbid. For houses priced at more than $150,000, there are no general rules to go by. Things are wide open, with some being bought for as much as 50 percent under the asking price.

The price a house will sell for depends much on current market conditions, including the availability of mortgage money. If mortgages are easy to obtain, people can often buy a house they otherwise could not buy. The state of the stock market is also a factor. When the market is going well, it exerts a favorable psychological influence and it indicates both general prosperity and a greater number of people with money. Conversely, a sluggish stock market has the opposite effects.

The sale price also depends on such things as whether or not an owner is in a hurry to sell. In sum, it comes down to supply and demand, as with other products for sale. Such facts are good to remember when you shop for a house. They can give you a sixth sense for the values of houses.

■ MAKING THE OFFER

Let's say you've decided on a house to buy. You've investigated it carefully; its price is within your range and is consistent with market values. You will have to put your offer in writing. It is possible that there may be some back and forth with the seller before you have formalized your offer in a signed agreement. You may even have agreed on price. But, as the saying goes, your deal isn't worth the paper it's written on. It is time to tread carefully now. If accepted, your offer becomes a legally binding contract. You should have a real estate lawyer review the purchase contract before it is submitted to the seller. Although you often have a grace period where adjustments can be made, things will go more smoothly if you involve your lawyer first.

When you make the offer, it is traditional to put up some funds as an act of good faith. This deposit is often called *earnest money*, as it demonstrates that you are serious, or earnest, about purchasing the property. The more money you put up as a deposit, the more attractive your offer will appear to the seller. So in an active market, where it's probable you could be competing with other buyers, you may want to make a large deposit. Your real estate agent may tell you to put up 5 percent of your offering price, but it's probably not necessary to go so high. Though it's common for these deposits to run from 1 percent to 3 percent of the offering price, there is no hard and fast rule as to what the amount should be. Because there is always a possibility that you could lose the money, don't put up more than is necessary. The right deposit is the most money the buyer is willing to give and the least the seller is willing to take. In addition, it is risky to actually give the money to the seller. There is always the chance that if the deal falls through you will have difficulty recovering the money and may even have to pay a lawyer to handle it. Rather, you should have your real estate agent hold the money in a trust account or in escrow. If you cannot come to terms, or if the deal falls through due to no fault of your own, you should get the money back. One of the functions of the purchase contract is to stipulate how such a situation will be handled. When your offer is accepted, these funds will be disbursed to the seller. In general the transfer of funds tends to make an agreement binding because it displays mutual consent. Also, this money is a deposit. When you are at the closing table, the money counts toward your purchase price, it is not a seller's bonus.

The contract does much more than specify price. It also outlines terms. Price is usually of utmost importance to the seller, so it may be a good negotiating strategy to acquiesce to the seller's price in return for more attractive terms. For instance, you may get the seller to cover some or all of your closing costs or even offer some financing. The contract will also specify what personal property, such as major appliances, may be included in the purchase.

The offer will generally include contingencies that require the completion of an act or event before the contract is binding. A typical contingency is that you will obtain a mortgage. But this clause has to be precisely worded specifying the amount of time you will have to secure the funds, the interest rate, perhaps the type of mortgage. There may also be a contingency that you have to sell your home. Again, a time period would be specified. You may make your offer conditional on occupancy by a certain date. Buyers who are dependent on funds from a third party, such as a generous relative, may make their offer contingent on that person's approval. The more contingencies you have and the more formidable they appear, the less attractive your offer will be to the seller. Therefore, you can put yourself in a better position with a letter of preapproval for financing. Even so, you may want to give yourself an out, because rates can change rapidly and you can never be absolutely certain about financing until funds are secured. But in this scenario you could specify a maximum interest rate well above the prevailing rate, and that would not be so threatening to the sellers. Similarly, if you have already sold your current home, you do not have to worry about scaring off homesellers by making the sale of their property contingent on the sale of yours, a real dealbreaker, particularly in a sluggish market. A lawyer can be a big help with contingencies, ensuring that they are properly worded to give you the best options without being overly threatening to the seller.

One very important contingency that has become more or less standard is that the property must satisfactorily pass whatever professional inspection or inspections you see necessary. The inspector may see faults that you will want to address as required repairs for the seller to make or as a reduction in price. If a major problem is uncovered, you can probably get out of the agreement altogether.

In many transactions there will be some back and forth once you have made your offer. Keep track of where your obligations are as negotiations proceed, and ask your attorney for advice if you're in any way confused. For instance, if the seller counteroffers, your offer has in effect been declined. It is therefore your right, if you desire, to withdraw from negotiations, and you are entitled to your full deposit.

■ NEGOTIATING FOR A HOUSE

Because negotiating is not commonplace in our culture, we often feel uncomfortable doing it. The one commonplace setting for negotiating is the automobile dealership. There the hardball and manipulative tactics of salespeople and their managers leaves such a bitter taste with so many people that it is now becoming a trend in the auto industry to set prices that are nonnegotiable and purportedly fair. Other settings for negotiation are garage sales, resale shops, flea markets and antiques stores. To the many who frequent these outlets, the back and forth of negotiating is half the fun. However, in a home purchase stakes run high. After all, you are spending thousands of dollars, assuming large and long-term debt, and making a relatively illiquid investment. It is natural to be a little nervous, particularly if you are new to the game. There are plenty of good books on the topic of negotiating in general that can be of help; one of the best is *Getting to Yes*, by Roger Fisher and William Ury (Viking Penguin, 1991).

In general, if you follow the advice of this chapter, you should do fine. Make sure you know your market, formulate a buying strategy (and stick to the plan) and gather as much information as you can about the circumstances of the seller. Keep a level head during negotiations. This is sometimes easier said than done during a home purchase, for both the buyer and the seller because there is an emotional attachment to the home. The common advice of not falling in love with a home is unrealistic because you at least have a serious attraction by the time you're ready to plop down your life savings to buy it. More precisely, you should try to conceal your love for the home. Basic negotiating advice is to be willing to walk away from the deal. If you lose your head during a time of offers and counteroffers, it's easy to pay too much. Part of your plan should be setting in mind a top price you're willing to pay, based on all the information you've collected in the market. Don't lose sight of that top price as negotiations proceed. Also, although the theme of this chapter is to avoid paying too much for a house, look at negotiations as an opportunity as well. Extrapolating from Poor Richard's aphorism that a penny saved is a penny earned, you'll rarely get a chance to "earn" several thousand dollars so easily as when you're negotiating for a house.

There is no such thing as a typical negotiating process. Nevertheless, it is useful to recount a story of one home transaction as a way to illustrate some of the ideas of this chapter in action. While you're looking for homes, ask friends and relatives or even your agent for their war stories.

Charlie and Mary, parents with three young children, owned a home that they felt would not be big enough for their growing brood. They liked their neighborhood, though they had some reservations about schools. They started looking around for homes in a few nearby suburbs. Because Mary was at home during the day, she did most of the looking, particularly in the hours her two eldest children were in school. Charlie and Mary had agreed that it was time to make a long-term decision on where they would live. They agreed that they would look for homes through the spring and early summer while they discussed with an architect possibilities for an addition to their current home. If by July they had not found another home, they would begin work on an addition.

Mary had been keeping an eye out for homes in their desired areas for some time. A few friends who lived there would tell her if they saw something good on the market. Now with a deadline in sight, Mary stepped up her efforts. She had been using a real estate agent named Stephanie, whom a friend had recommended, and now she began working more closely with her. Stephanie worked with them in the traditional manner, as a subagent of the seller. As it happened, it was one of Mary's scouts, not Stephanie, who tipped Mary off to the home on which they would bid. Mary called Stephanie to ask her to arrange a showing. After viewing the home, Mary had Stephanie show her houses for sale in the immediate vicinity. She also asked Stephanie to run off a list of selling prices of comparable houses in the area that had recently changed hands. Together they drove by the homes on the list. Mary concluded that the home was fairly priced. She was ready to take quick action. Mary took a second look at the home, this time with her husband Charlie, and they were ready to make an offer.

They went with Stephanie to her office to draw up a purchase agreement. The sellers were asking $320,000. The home was offered for sale under an exempt listing, meaning that there could be no sign posted in the front yard and that the listing broker could not put the property up on the MLS. Mary had learned that the owners were going to be moving overseas due to job relocation. Charlie and Mary had gone through five home negotiations including both purchases and sales. More importantly, negotiating was a routine aspect of Charlie's daily work, so he felt quite comfortable in the process. Charlie's philosophy was to always leave plenty of room for negotiating up. He decided to offer

$290,000. Privately, Charlie and Mary had agreed that they were willing to pay the asking price to get the house. But they did not think they would have to. They were confident they would be able to get the property for $310,000.

Stephanie was not pleased with Charlie's initial offer. She argued that the home was priced fairly, if not low, a fact Mary also knew to be true (but she also knew enough to keep quiet, because Charlie always handled negotiations well). "The sellers will be insulted," Stephanie said, "I don't think they'll counter an offer like that." She suggested that Charlie offer $300,000. Charlie disagreed, feeling that if he offered $300,000, there would not be any room to negotiate. The sellers might stick to their price or come down only a few thousand. He also knew the house had been on the market for over a month. The exempt listing told him that the owners wanted to sell the house quietly and privately, that they did not want lots of people traipsing through. In addition, for whatever reason, the listing agent was from a suburb 15 miles away. Without the benefit of the MLS or a house sign, she was dependent entirely on word-of-mouth in an area where she was not active. Even with his offer low, Charlie felt the owner might be eager to talk. And if not, well Charlie didn't usually sweat that kind of thing out. He was happy enough in his present home.

Charlie stuck to his price of $290,000, but he made the offer attractive in other ways. He waived common contingencies. He knew he could qualify for the mortgage he needed, so he struck the contingency on approval of a mortgage. Because the owner wanted to occupy the home until June and he felt confident he could sell his own home in four months, he did not tie the offer to the sale of his own home. Finally, he attached a check for $2,000 to be presented with the purchase contract. He wanted the owners to know that they were serious and that they were ready to talk.

Stephanie came back with news that the owner had said that "he wasn't so good at this kind of thing" and countered with $306,000 suggesting they split the difference. It was exactly what Charlie had expected. "You better take it," Stephanie added. Now Charlie and Mary had already done better than the price they had set their sights on. Maybe it was the way Stephanie had phrased the counteroffer, Charlie felt there was still room for play. He offered $300,000. "Tell them I'm not good at this either," he said.

Stephanie was exasperated. "Well what price will you take the home at?" That is the loaded question in the real estate transaction. If Charlie answered the question, Stephanie's fiduciary obligation would be to disclose that figure to the sellers when she presented Charlie's offer. As a buyer, you have to assume that she will honor that duty. Charlie phrased his answer astutely, "Don't indicate that we will go any higher."

"Oh, don't worry," Stephanie responded, "I'm working for you. I'm on your side." Charlie liked to hear that and felt confident things were going their way. Mary didn't like it, because she didn't think it was true. By the rules of agency, it clearly was not true. Here's a good example of where the practice of real estate makes the theory of agency and subagency a little fuzzy. Was Stephanie indeed on Charlie and Mary's side? Only she can answer that, but our guess is that she was thinking, "I've got these sides so close, I've got to make this deal." Stephanie did get the sale, and Charlie and Mary got the home for $300,000.

Charlie and Mary did their homework. They understood the market, had a good idea of the worth of the house they bid on and were able to get it at an excellent price. But no matter how good a price you can negotiate, you want to avoid buying the low-quality house. The following chapters describe in detail how to judge the design and structural quality of a house.

The Unforeseen Expenses of Buying and Owning a House

A young couple appeared at the bank on their closing day to consummate the purchase of their first house. They sat at a big table with the seller, lawyers and other people they didn't know.

In the next two hours, papers shuffled back and forth, and they signed where their lawyer told them to. They were relieved of $8,600 of their money, over and above the price of the house they were buying. These documents contained a series of fees, one after the other, in addition to the price of the house they were buying. Each was for a separate item, paid for in cash. The total was nearly 5 percent of the house price ($175,000).

This forced expenditure, a hefty sum, is paid for what's called "closing costs," some of the largest unforeseen expenses that can hit you when you buy a house. Even for people who have bought houses before, closing costs are often unpredictably higher than anticipated.

Other expenses also can arise suddenly and painfully when you buy and own a house. They include such things as "points" paid for the mortgage, a special property tax assessment, or a sharp rise in school taxes, not to mention emergency service and maintenance repairs for new and old houses.

Such bills can mount up, though they need not. And they're not necessarily inevitable. They depend, of course, on such things as the house you are buying, where it's located and the mortgage obtained. Here are the most likely such expenses and what you can do to reduce them—and sometimes even eliminate them.

■ CONSIDER CLOSING COSTS FIRST

Closing costs, sometimes called settlement costs, are the admission fee you pay at the door before being allowed in to buy a house. They include charges associated with the transaction of buying a house and obtaining a mortgage. They also include other charges that have, it seems, no other purpose than soaking the homebuyer and feathering somebody's vested-interest nest.

They go for a variety of items, small and sometimes large. They can range from as little as a several hundred dollars (if you're fortunate) up to 6 percent of the house price. They are not unlike paying for a new car and then being charged another $500 or more to get the keys for it and drive it home. Except the charge is a lot more for a house.

In the 1970s lenders came under fire for excessive closing fees. The Real Estate Settlements Procedure Act (RESPA) gives some help to consumers, with specific requirements that ensure that both buyer and seller are informed about charges. Within 24 hours of your mortgage application, the lender must provide you with the U.S. Department of Housing and Urban Development (HUD) booklet (or their own equivalent) entitled "Settlement Costs and You." It includes a general discussion of closing costs, including a line-by-line explanation of the Uniform Settlement Statement, a standard HUD form used at closing. At the same time, most lenders will also provide you with a good faith estimate of all the closing costs. They are required to do so within 72 hours of application.

Below is a list of charges a buyer might see at the closing table:

- Application fee
- Title insurance
- Hazard insurance
- Prorated taxes
- Prorated interest
- Appraisal fee
- Escrow or attorney fee
- Credit report
- Survey
- Pest inspection
- Underwriting
- Lender inspection fee
- Lender's attorney fee
- Recording
- Document preparation
- Notary
- Courier
- Assumption fees (if you're assuming a loan)
- Property transfer tax (in some localities)

It's reasonable to question all charges, but the time to do it is not at the closing table. Your lender must give you the estimated charges at least three days before the close. Ask if you can get a list of charges earlier, and take the time to review them. There may be mistakes. For instance, a fee you negotiated with the sellers to pay may turn up as a charge to you. If any of the lender's charges seem unreasonable, you should ask for an explanation before closing day.

Some of the costs you'll pay are obviously important and necessary. You know you want hazard insurance and title insurance. It's reasonable that the lender will order an appraisal of the property. But other fees will border on the ridiculous, what borrowers call "junk fees" and lenders call by a dozen different names. Here is a rundown of what closing costs consist of and what can be done to reduce them.

Application fee.   It's also called a mortgage commitment fee or service charge. It usually pays for the house appraisal, home buyer credit check and other loan processing costs. Some lenders and builders absorb part or all of such charges because they're considered part of the work for issuing you a mortgage, or because they want your business. Others charge, it seems, as much as the traffic will bear. An application fee can range from as little as a few hundred dollars up to a flat 1 percent or so of the mortgage amount.

Its total can also depend on the availability of mortgages at a given time. If they are in tight supply, the cost of obtaining one goes up. If mortgage money is plentiful, lenders may vie for your business and may absorb part or all of the fee. When you shop for a mortgage, merely hinting that you may go elsewhere for your mortgage may prompt lenders to give you a break. It depends on how much they want your business. Sometimes negotiating will persuade the seller of the house to pay a portion of this bill, as well as other closing costs. This, too, depends on how much the seller wants to sell and how able a negotiator the buyer is.

Title search and insurance.   Title companies thoroughly examine the chain of title and all public records affecting the property to make sure that the seller has a clear title to the property being sold. If the search shows that the title is insurable, the title company will issue a policy protecting the holder from any loss due to defects in the title or any liens or encumbrances on the property. Mortgage lenders usually require a title insurance policy to protect their interest in the property should questions about the title arise. Title search and insurance may be bought separately or in a package. Title insurance rates are generally set by a state's insurance department, but the cost of a title search can vary. Checking on this and shopping for your own title search often can save money. Remember, sometimes a title search is quickly done by a lawyer sending a law clerk to the county court house for a quick check of the files. In addition, you need not always buy both title insurance and title search from the title insurance company.

There are two kinds of title policies. The first, the lender's policy, protects the mortgage lender only and is mandatory. The second, the owner's policy, is optional. It protects you, the buyer, in case of a flaw in the title for the house. For your own protection, you should get owner's title insurance, even if an attorney or title company search shows the title is good.

In many areas of the country, it's customary for the seller of the house to pay for the title insurance. That makes sense, considering that the seller should vouch for the title to the property being sold. In other areas, the title search and insurance fee are subject to bargaining between buyer and seller. The seller, including some builders, can often be induced to absorb part of the expense. In still other cases, the buyer pays.

You may have some choice of title company. The escrow company or lender may have a favorite company because of perks or outright kickbacks. Any explicit relationship should be disclosed to you by the RESPA. Fees average about 0.5 percent of the cost of the house. Ask the lender about using another title company if charges are extraordinarily high.

Lawyer fees.   This can stir resentment, particularly when homebuyers are charged by the lender for the lender's lawyer fee in addition to the fee paid to their own lawyer. But money for your own lawyer can be well spent. Lawyer fees can range from a few hundred dollars up to about $600 or more, varying according to the level of services and where you are. It's wise to involve a lawyer as early as possible, ideally before you sign a purchase agreement, so you can truly benefit from the legal counsel. Don't try to save money by hiring a lawyer only for the close. There won't be time for the lawyer to examine the details, and problems might go unnoticed. And even if they are caught, do you really want to deal with an easement problem, for instance, at the closing table? Shopping for a lawyer can save you a pretty penny. Besides, the legal work may be tedious, perhaps, but it's usually routine, taking no special talent or effort. Do, however, choose only a lawyer who specializes in real estate. Any other lawyer should be shunned for the same reason that anyone with a heart condition would do well to consult only a heart specialist. In addition, lawyers specializing in real estate will run an efficient operation, using paralegals or secretaries for routine work and follow-up with other parties, and may therefore offer a more competitive rate. Ask your real estate agent for a recommendation. Sometimes agents refer lots of clients to a lawyer, who will offer an attractive rate in return. And again, like most other closing costs, lawyers' fees can also be negotiable. If not, try another lawyer. There are plenty eager for work.

"Points." Sometimes confused with the loan origination fee, which is often measured in percentage points, a point is basically a charge relating to the mortgage itself. It can also be the single largest closing cost charge of all.

One point is 1 percent of the mortgage being obtained. The total points charged can run as high as 6 or 7 points—in other words, up to 7 percent of the mortgage. Those aren't small potatoes. The lower the interest rate on your mortgage, the larger the potential points charge. It's a charge to compensate lenders for the difference they will receive in interest on the mortgage, compared with the interest they could receive investing the same money somewhere else at the prevailing market rate. Points can also be called "discount" points, because the charge is basically an upfront fee that lowers your mortgage interest rate as compared to current levels. You have some choice as to how many points you pay, and Chapter 3 provides advice for comparison shopping. Points, too, are negotiable with the seller of a house who may absorb a portion of this charge.

Mortgage insurance and prorated interest.   You might also pay a premium for mortgage insurance, required if the mortgage loan exceeds 80 percent of the house value or if a Federal Housing Administration (FHA) mortgage is obtained. This protects the lender against loss if you fail to make the payments. Don't confuse it with mortgage life or disability insurance that can pay off your mortgage in case of death or disability and that you may obtain at your option at any time. Also common is a prorated interest charge. Interest is usually paid in arrears. For instance, your June 1 payment covers interest for the month of May. You'll probably have to pay the prorated share of the current month's interest at closing.

Taxes and escrow money.   Buy a house and you must pay property taxes, your share of city, county, state and local school costs. They are usually paid annually or twice a year, thus have already been paid by the sellers of the house up to the next payment date. You then must reimburse the sellers for their part of these taxes paid in advance. Your share, paid on closing day, is prorated from the date of purchase to the next due date for each tax.

Escrow money is what you prepay, in monthly install-ments, for future taxes and sometimes for homeowners insurance. They're paid to your mortgage lender. That's to soften the blow when a large lump-sum tax payment is due. The mortgage lender may require a portion of this money in advance, on closing day, as a head start on the next tax pay-ment. State and local transfer taxes also must be paid for certain parts of the home buying transaction.

Hazard insurance.   First, there's a hazard insurance policy (covering physical damage due to fire, windstorm or flood). It's usually the only insurance required by a mortgage lender. Insurance for theft and liability are also desirable.

All three can be obtained in a homeowner's policy. This offers better all-around total coverage (for less money) than obtaining individual hazard, theft and liability policies.

Incidentally, a few banks and other mortgage lenders would have you believe that you must take the insurance they sell. It's part of the mortgage package, they say. Not only is this coercive selling—it is also against the law in many states. You do have the right to get your own insurance—although, of course, it should be adequate for the house. Buy insurance that covers 100% of the replacement costs, not just the market value. It's more expensive but worth it. Or, at the very least, it should cover 80 percent of the house replacement cost.

You can check the financial stability of insurance companies through A.M. Best or Standard & Poors. Also, once a year, the magazine *Consumer Reports* ranks companies based on customer satisfaction. You might save money by using the same company for car, home and life insurance.

Miscellaneous costs.   These may include costs for such things as a property survey, photographs of the house and, of all things, heating oil left in the oil tank. If a survey is required, ask the seller for his last survey (often acceptable) or at least for partial payment of a new survey. Rather than pay a professional photographer's rate for photographs, you might provide them yourself. Nuisance bills for such things as unused oil are still (again) negotiable. After all, suppose you decide to convert to gas heat?

To sum up, brace yourself for closing costs. The importance of shopping for reasonable closing costs, as well as a desirable mortgage, cannot be overemphasized. Remember that various items of your closing costs are obtainable from different sources, as well as being negotiable. Get an estimate for all when you first arrange for a mortgage. Why do lenders bother with these small charges when they make thousands of dollars in interest? The lender will probably sell the loan and use the fees to offset the cost of processing the loan. Look out for excessive fees with vague names. You may question every one. If saving dollars is important, shopping around carefully can pay off very well. Home-builders selling houses often can offer better-than-usual terms and prices at group rates. That's not always true, so it can pay to shop and compare. If negotiating and bargaining for low closing costs is not your cup of tea, hire a good, no-nonsense real estate lawyer who can do it for you.

■ UNFORESEEN TAX HIKES

The property taxes on a house may run up to several thousand dollars a year, depending on the assessed valuation of the house and the local tax rate. That's how you pay for local services, including fire and police protection as well as schools, water and sewers. It's up to you to determine what they are before you buy. Don't, however, necessarily rely on the casual word of a builder's salesperson or a real estate broker. Find out from the local tax assessor's office. Should you buy a used house, ask to see the owner's most recent tax bills. There are usually separate bills for school taxes, village and/or town taxes, and county and state property taxes.

An increase in taxes is least likely if you buy a house in an established area where few new services and no new schools will be needed. They are more likely when you move into a growing new area or a new development or both. If new schools, roads, sewers and other facilities will be needed, taxes are sure to go up, and you must pay your share. It's as simple as that. The greater the local growth expected, the greater the future tax bill to be expected.

An across-the-board hike in the local real estate tax rate is generally the way you pay for expanded services, such as more police and fire protection and new schools. In addition, there are "special assessments" levied on property owners to pay for capital improvements, such as new water mains, sidewalks and curbs, new street paving, a garbage plant, even streetlights and fire hydrants and, usually most expensive of all, a new sewer system for a community. Not all of these can be foreseen, but also remember that they are generally the result of vocal public demand, rather than arbitrary decisions by government officials.

Being hit with a series of such bills can make things financially tough for you, especially if they come on top of homeownership bills that are already as high as your income will allow. Realistically speaking, therefore, it is a good idea to allow a cushion in your budget to pay for possible tax hikes if you buy a house in a new development or in a rapidly growing area. A visit to the local tax assessor's office can shed light on the prospects for new taxes. How much are the local real estate taxes expected to rise in the future? What about the likelihood of special assessments in the area? Don't be fooled if someone tells you taxes can't go up because there's a legal ceiling to the tax rate. New services cost money, and the local government can boost taxes by hiking all assessments without changing the tax base.

Just as closing costs have come under sharp attack, fast-climbing property taxes throughout the country have also brought cries of anguish from homeowners. Before you buy a house, therefore, inquire locally about the future prospects for the local property taxes. Are the local property taxes (especially for schools) likely to go up or down, and by how much as a result of possible court-mandated changes in how property taxes are levied?

■ NEW HOUSE EXPENSES

A man who bought a colonial house in a new development says, "The builder seeded the front lawn but only ten feet in the rear. We got only three bushes in front. A lawn for the rest of the property plus additional landscaping cost me $2,000 after we moved in."

Window screens and storm windows also may have to be bought, though insulated double-pane glass windows are becoming increasingly common in new houses. You will also need window shades and curtains, perhaps new appliances and (even though not essential) such things as an attic fan or a privacy fence around the patio. There can be unexpected expenses for new storage cabinets or closet expansion and changes or additions here and there to make the house more suitable.

The biggest potential expenses in a new house are those you must pay to correct major design or construction shortcomings. You may find, for example, that the kitchen requires drastic changes or expansion to make it work. Or a new bathroom is essential. Occasionally things go wrong with the house, and the builder cannot or will not repair them. These are clearly the expensive big-ticket items to avoid, and avoiding them calls for a thorough check on the design and construction of the house before you buy.

■ POSSIBLE UNFORESEEN EXPENSES WITH A USED HOUSE

The most costly unforeseen expenses with a used house are due to old age and obsolescence. In time, the water heater or furnace stops running, the structure requires a new roof, or other repairs are necessary. But again, being prepared for them requires a good check on the house before buying (detailed in Chapter 7).

A used house will often need new interior painting and redecorating; of course, doing these yourself can save money. New window curtains are usually needed (but unlike a new house, window screens and storm windows often come with the house). Find out about this beforehand. On the bright side, a used house usually has a lawn and is landscaped, so these items should not bring on unforeseen expenses.

The various expenses that we've just noted should not necessarily frighten you. Sometimes they will shrink to very little, particularly if you've scouted the house carefully before buying. So don't be scared by imagined bills, and don't necessarily put off buying a house because of fears—unless justified, of course.

It is also good, however, to set aside money you are likely to need to pay for settling into the house you buy, because there is one last big expense trap to avoid: the high interest rates on installment loans that people must take out in order to pay for unforeseen expenses. That brings up the importance of knowing what you can spend for a house.

■ HOW MUCH HOUSE CAN YOU AFFORD?

An old rule that is still bandied about is that you can afford a house priced up to two and a half times your annual income. A person earning $40,000 a year therefore could buy a house priced up to $100,000.

But that rule can be way off. Use it at your own peril. It overlooks the fact that property taxes can run several hundred dollars a year for one house, but two to three times that amount for another house at exactly the same price. It makes no allowance for heating that can run hundreds of dollars a month in the North and practically nothing for a similar house in the South. Nor does it allow for mortgage interest rates and carrying charges that are considerably higher today than when that mossbacked old rule of thumb was first used.

Some people may spend up to three times their annual income for a house, whereas others should not spend a penny more than twice their income and sometimes even less. The amount you can afford will depend far more on the monthly carrying costs, upkeep and ownership expenses for a particular house than on the ratio of the house sales price to your income.

Mortgage lenders do, by necessity, use certain oversimplified rules. One common rule in use in recent years was that you could qualify for a home mortgage by spending up to 28 percent of your gross income for the monthly carrying costs of a house. That's the sum of money spent each month for mortgage principal, interest, property taxes and insurance. Your total debt including housing costs and all other debt payments can be up to 36 percent of monthly income. The exact qualifying ratios can vary by lender.

These lender guidelines are established minimums. More accurately, how much you can afford to spend for a house depends on your income minus what you must spend each month for all other essential outlays. Think of all your monthly expenditures for ongoing services and items. If you use a computer program to handle personal finances these numbers will be readily available. Otherwise keep a notebook for a few weeks and record all your expenditures as a way to pick up spending patterns. Then fill in Figure 2.1.

Figure 2.2 is a factor table for a 15-year loan or a 30-year loan at various interest rates. Use the factor at a given interest rate and loan term to determine the monthly payment in principal and interest for every $1,000 borrowed. For instance, if you were borrowing $140,000 at an 8 percent interest rate on a 30-year loan, your monthly principal and interest payment would be:

$$\$140 \times 7.34 = \$1,027.60$$

To figure how large a loan your available monthly payment would get you, start with the total mortgage and interest payment from the bottom of the worksheet in Figure 2.1. Locate the factor for your interest rate and term. Divide your monthly principal and interest by the factor; then, to get the total mortgage amount, multiply by 1,000. For example, if you can afford a monthly principal and interest payment of $950, and you plan on a 30-year mortgage at 7.5 percent,

$$\$950 \div 6.99 = \$135.908$$

$$\$135.908 \times 1,000 = \$135,908.$$

The maximum mortgage you could afford would be about $136,000. How large a mortgage you can qualify for is a matter for lenders to decide according to their guidelines.

FIGURE 2.1 ■ Household Expenses Worksheet

1. ADD UP YOUR MONTHLY LIVING EXPENSES OTHER THAN FOR HOUSING:

Food	$ _____
Clothing	_____
Medical and dental bills	_____
Life and health insurance	_____
Other insurance	_____
Automobile upkeep and insurance	_____
Commuting to work	_____
Entertainment and recreation	_____
Children's school, college expenses	_____
Installment payments, (washer, dryer, other monthly installment payments)	_____
Church and other contributions	_____
Vacation	_____
Hobbies, books, magazines, records	_____
Savings, investments, etc.	_____
Personal gifts, Christmas, Holiday expenses	_____
Miscellaneous (barber, beauty shop expenses, bathroom supplies)	_____
Any other?	_____
Total living expenses other than for housing	$ _____

FIGURE 2.1 ■ Household Expenses Worksheet (Continued)

2. DETERMINE MONEY AVAILABLE FOR HOUSING:

Total gross monthly income
for household $ _____

Deductions for income taxes,
Social Security, etc.   – _____

Net take-home pay   _____

Less living expenses   – _____

Total monthly money available
for housing $ _____

3. DETERMINE MONEY AVAILABLE FOR MONTHLY
PRINCIPAL AND INTEREST PAYMENTS:

Total monthly money available for
housing from line above $ _____

Subtract amount estimated for property
taxes, insurance, and monthly heating,
upkeep, and operating costs. This figure
will vary according to the house and
where you live and must be estimated
locally.   _____

Later, when you have settled on a house
you may buy, an accurate determination
of insurance, taxes and other monthly
ownership costs for the house should be
entered here.   _____

Total money left for monthly mortgage
principal and interest payments $ _____

FIGURE 2.2 ■ Monthly Payment Factors

Interest rate	15-year	30-year
5.0%	7.91	5.37
5.5%	8.17	5.68
6.0%	8.44	6.00
6.5%	8.71	6.32
7.0%	8.99	6.65
7.5%	9.27	6.99
8.0%	9.56	7.34
8.5%	9.85	7.69
9.0%	10.14	8.05
9.5%	10.44	8.41
10.0%	10.75	8.78
10.5%	11.05	9.15
11.0%	11.52	9.71

■ HOW MUCH CASH IS NEEDED TO BUY A HOUSE?

First there's the down payment and closing costs and then cash on the barrelhead for moving and the settling-in expenses reported in this chapter. You may have plans for redecorating or renovations. In addition to the money needed for these inevitable bills, it's usually a good idea to have a reserve cash cushion. How much of a cushion depends on the unforeseen expenses that may confront you. On reading this far you should have a good idea of what they may or may not be.

The down payment required and what you must spend monthly to repay the mortgage depend on how the house is financed.

■ ═══ CHAPTER 3 ═══ ■

The Tight
Mortgage Bind

Not long ago, choosing the right mortgage was a breeze—fixed rate, 30 years, take it or leave it. Even the adjustable-rate mortgage is a relative newcomer, devised when banks were paying high interest rates on deposits while servicing mortgages originated years earlier at much lower rates. Banks introduced adjustable-rate mortgages as a way to minimize their risk in a period of rising interest rates. Borrowers enjoy the same benefit of flexibility and can hope for their upside of declining rates.

Choosing between adjustable and fixed rates is just one of many decisions you must make when selecting a mortgage. You'll also have to decide the number of points to pay up front. Another common choice today is between the 15-year mortgage and the traditional 30-year term. You may also wish to look at Federal Housing Administration (FHA) loans that, contrary to common perception, are not for low-income people only. If you are a qualified veteran, the Department of Veterans Affairs offers the excellent VA loan program.

Lenders are constantly coming up with new variations on loans. Of course, it is not a sense of charity that is driving banks to devise these different mortgage products. Nevertheless, it is only to the homebuyer's advantage to have more choices. You now have the opportunity to select a mortgage that is more appropriate to your financial situation. You could save thousands of dollars. The trick is to make the right choice; the alternative may be getting caught in a mortgage bind.

Here is a typical example of a poor choice made by first-time homebuyers, a young couple, double-income, no kids. The wife was the bigger wage earner of the family, working as a consultant in a large firm. Prospects were good for the young man to gain a big income increase in the near future. He was a sales rep for a high-tech firm, moving quite successfully through their advancement track and in position to land a potentially lucrative territory in the next year. When choosing a mortgage, the couple preferred stability and went for the fixed rate. A couple years after purchasing the home interest rates went down to 6 percent, 3 points below their 9 percent mortgage. Meanwhile, the husband's income had nearly doubled. It made sense to refinance, and they did, because the amount they would pay for their points and closing costs would be earned back in interest savings in about 18 months. Fortunately, qualifying was a snap because their income was better than ever. However, the couple regretted that they had not chosen an adjustable-rate mortgage in the beginning because they would have enjoyed a lower interest rate without spending a few thousand dollars to refinance. Indeed, they were always good candidates to risk an adjustable-rate mortgage because they were confident that their income would increase significantly.

Theirs is not such a sorry story; it's easy to absorb a mistake when times are good. The worst-case scenario is if you find yourself with a mortgage that exceeds the market value of the house. Certain mortgages risk negative amortization, causing such a scenario, or it might happen if you are highly leveraged and housing values in your area drop rapidly. Then you are truly in a mortgage bind. Without enough funds from the sale of the house to pay off the mortgage, you may be stuck in a house that you'd really rather sell.

Most people are not as careful in selecting a mortgage as they are in choosing a home to purchase, though in purely financial terms the mortgage is more important. After all, it's probably worth anywhere from 80 percent to 90 percent of the value of the home. This chapter will present an overview of your mortgage choices with some warnings about potential pitfalls. You may want to go to your bookstore or library and get a book specifically on mortgages.

■ COMPARISON SHOPPING

The most basic mortgage advice is to put some time and energy into comparison shopping. Follow the mortgage rates in the local paper for a few weeks and choose a few lenders who are consistently competitive. When you're ready to actually apply, call around. Get names of lenders from friends or relatives. Don't look just to banks—credit unions, insurance companies, even individuals are also potential lenders. Also, remember rates will change daily. So canvass your lenders over a short period of time, preferably all on the same day. Perhaps you'll want to use a mortgage broker who has a good idea of what's available but who will likely charge you more in points or fees. When you call lenders, ask a lot of questions. The goal is to eliminate surprises and compare using a range of criteria. Don't choose a mortgage purely because of the lowest rate. There are other factors—fees, servicing policies, points—just to name a few.

As you read the advice in this chapter, you'll see that it will be much easier to make decisions if you have a good idea of how long you'll stay in the property. Depending on your circumstances, it could be hard to be precise, but the issue deserves some serious thought. Another consideration is patterns of income you can predict, such as the case of the example above. Are you a two-income couple who plan on dropping to a single income in a few years when you have children? Are your kids getting closer to college age? Would you like to start your own business in a few years? In a world that's changing as fast as ours, it's hard to know where you'll be even in five years. But if you do have a plan, be sure to take it into account as you select a mortgage.

■ THE MORTGAGE BASICS

For a first-time homebuyer, shopping for a mortgage can be like visiting a foreign country. It's really not all that hard to get around in lending land, but there are a few words and concepts to learn.

A big player in setting the rules of the mortgage game is the Federal National Mortgage Association (FNMA), commonly called Fannie Mae. Most mortgages are bought and sold on the secondary market, and the Fannie Mae is by far the largest secondary market purchaser. They set the minimum standards for loans that most lenders will follow in order to have a marketable commodity.

Before you even begin shopping for homes, you should have a general idea of how large a mortgage you can qualify for. Lenders use two qualifying ratios to determine the credit worthiness of borrowers: *housing debt* and *total debt*.

Housing debt = Monthly housing payment
÷ Total monthly income

Total debt = (Monthly housing payment + All other monthly
obligations) ÷ Total monthly income

Your monthly housing payment consists of Principal, Interest, Taxes and Insurance (homeowners) (PITI). Examples of your monthly obligations that enter into your total debt would be credit card debt (minimum monthly payment due), car loans, student loans, alimony, child support, etc. Generally the maximum ratios for a conventional mortgage are 28 percent for housing debt and 36 percent for total debt. There are special programs that allow you to exceed these ratios, some of which we'll discuss later in the chapter. Again, Fannie Mae sets these ratios. They are subject to change, and individual lenders may use different ratios.

You've probably considered how large a down payment you want to make for the purchase. The down payment will determine your *Loan-to-Value ratio* (LTV). Expressed as a percentage, the LTV is simply the mortgage amount divided by the value of the house. If you're buying a house worth $150,000 and borrowing $120,000, your LTV is 80 percent and you're putting 20 percent down ($30,000).

Although it is possible these days to purchase a home with an LTV as high as 95 percent, for conventional loans you will probably need to purchase *private mortgage insurance* (PMI) for any loan with an LTV of more than 80 percent. PMI insures the lender against some of the losses of a high-risk loan that goes sour. The borrower pays the premium. Costs and payment plans vary. There may be an up-front fee and then a fraction of a percent added to each month's payment.

Typically, you will see mortgage rates quoted with an interest rate and *points*. As discussed in Chapter 1, points are a fee you (or if you successfully negotiate for it, the seller) pays at closing, measured in percentage points of the total loan amount. A mortgage of $100,000 with 2 points will cost $2,000 at closing. Lenders will use points to discount a mortgage, that is, for a larger up-front charge, they will offer a lower interest rate on a mortgage. For this reason, points are sometimes referred to as discount points. Any one lender will probably give you a few different choices of constructing a loan. The arrangement is great for the homebuyer because, in effect, you can tailor your own rate within a range. But it does make for some confusion when comparing mortgages.

The key concept in comparing various interest rate and points combinations is the *annual percentage rate* (APR). Truth in Lending laws require the lenders to disclose the APR shortly after you apply for the loan. But that's too late for comparison shopping. Always ask your lender up front what it will be. The APR is an expression of the true interest rate, factoring in the amount of points and credit fees (there is usually an origination fee as well) paid up front and averaging them over the term of the loan.

However, just because a mortgage comes in with a lower APR doesn't mean it's a better deal for you. Chances are you won't keep the mortgage for the full term of the loan. Paying points up front for a lower rate makes more sense the longer you plan to stay in the house. One short-hand way to compare this feature is to determine the dollar amount of points you'll pay, the monthly savings from the lower rate, and how long it will take you to break even. This ignores a host of other factors, such as tax ramifications, but is a basis for a broad-brush comparison.

Thomas Steinmetz, in his book *The Mortgage Kit* (Dearborn Financial Publishing), suggests the following formula for a rough estimate of the APR:

$$APR = \text{Quoted rate} + (\text{Number of points} \div 6)$$

If you plan to stay in the house more than 12 years, divide by 8; if 4 to 6 years, divide by 4; if less than 4 years, divide by the number of years.

Another feature to consider is assumability. Some loans permit *simple assumption*, meaning that when you sell, your buyer can take on your mortgage without having to qualify. Other loans are assumable but require the new buyers to qualify. Assumability is a nice feature to have when it's time to sell the house. You potentially could get your equity out much quicker. All FHA and VA loans are assumable.

■ HOW LARGE A DOWN PAYMENT SHOULD YOU MAKE?

The biggest hurdle in home ownership for most first-time buyers today is scraping up enough money for a down payment. So you might be asking, "How much do I have to put down?" A big advantage to FHA and VA loan programs is that they allow buyers to put very little down, 3 percent or even less. In recent years there also have been affordable housing initiatives, sometimes called community homebuying programs, that allow buyers put just 3 percent down but require that they complete a home ownership educational program. Fannie Mae has what they call a 3-2 option, where qualified buyers can make a 5 percent down payment, with 3 percent from their own funds and 2 percent coming from other sources, such as gifts. These programs have been well received and are likely to continue in one form or another. Ask your real estate agent or local lenders about what's available.

In making a small down payment you are leveraging your property, you are using Other People's Money, as the late night real estate investment hawkers like to put it. Leverage is great when the market rises, but there is the downside risk to consider. If your down payment is too small and property appreciation is slow or falling, you may get caught in a mortgage bind. You may need to sell at a time when you owe more than the house is worth.

Many lenders offer borrowers conventional loans with either 10 percent or 20 percent down. If you go with the lower down payment, you will have to pay the PMI premium, raising your monthly payment. FHA and VA loans include their own insurance premium.

So far we've discussed low down payments. You may feel you should put down as much as you can on the theory that it is the financially correct thing to do. After all, the more cash paid for a house, the less the mortgage loan and the more you save on interest charges.

In addition to the PMI savings, a large down payment also may get you a lower interest rate, compared with the interest charged on the maximum mortgage for the same house. The proponents of a large down payment also state that it's a good thing to make a big investment in your house; it adds to your credit rating, making you financially stalwart. Your monthly payments will be smaller, improving your cash flow and, besides, buying a house is one of the best investments a person can make.

But there's another side to the story. A small down payment can make sense, too. Don't hasten to put all your spare cash into the down payment. Weigh the pros and cons first. A small down payment lets you keep cash in reserve for the expenses you may face after buying the house. Remember that money owed on a mortgage can be repaid at by far the lowest interest rate of virtually any consumer loan. It's much cheaper than later finding yourself in a bind and being forced to borrow with an installment loan at two to three times the interest rate.

Conserving your cash can mean other benefits, too. The larger your mortgage, the more you may save on income taxes because mortgage-interest payments are tax deductible. There are the possibly higher earnings on your capital if it is invested elsewhere, rather than in your house. So don't feel compelled to put every last dollar into the down payment on a house. For some it may be the financially proper thing to do. For you, the opposite may make more sense.

■ CHOOSING BETWEEN A 15-YEAR LOAN AND A 30-YEAR LOAN

Many lenders are offering mortgages with shorter terms, such as 15 years. These loans offer substantial interest savings to borrowers. For example, a loan of $100,000 at 9 percent over a 30-year term would carry interest charges totaling $289,800; the same loan over a 15-year term would cost $182,700 in interest. You would save more than $107,000 with the 15-year loan.

As an added incentive the interest rates are sometimes lower on 15-year loans. In actuality, you would therefore save even more in the above example. On the other hand, it will be more difficult to qualify for a 15-year loan because your payments will be higher, though not by as much as you might think. Your monthly principal and interest payment on a $100,000 mortgage at 9 percent on the 15-year would be $1,015, as opposed to $805 for the 30-year loan. For a lot of families that $210 will make all the difference in whether or not they qualify for the mortgage.

The larger monthly payment of a 15-year mortgage, attractive as the savings may be, could become a burden if you fall into tough times. There is a better option. First, confirm that the mortgage does not allow prepayment penalties, charges for paying off the loan before its maturity. Be sure to ask about these charges when you canvass lenders. Prepayment penalties are not allowed in FHA and VA loans.

If there are no prepayment penalties, you are free to tailor your own accelerated payment program. In the case of the above example, you could simply add $200 to every payment with instructions that it be applied to principal. (Be sure to check with your lender on their procedures for extra principal payments so credit is properly applied.) Another method is to apply a small additional amount with each payment, perhaps as little as $10, during the first year of the mortgage, and increase the extra payment incrementally through the term of the mortgage. The advantage of the prepayment method over shortening the mortgage term is the peace of mind of knowing that if trouble strikes you can go to the more comfortable payments based on the 30-year amortization.

■ CONVENTIONAL, FIXED-RATE MORTGAGES

The appeal of the conventional fixed-rate mortgage is its stability. It can be reassuring to know that your monthly payment of principal and interest will not rise for the life of the mortgage. The fixed-rate mortgage is recommended for people living on a fixed income, including retired people and others who can expect little or no income increase.

Conventional mortgages will appeal to people who have enough cash for a down payment. At a minimum, you will need 5 percent of the purchase price for the down payment; most loans will require 10 or 20 percent. Conventional mortgages usually carry a slightly higher interest rate than adjustable-rate mortgages, because lenders want protection against rate increases just as consumers do. The higher rate means a larger monthly payment, making it more difficult to qualify for a conventional mortgage.

■ ADJUSTABLE-RATE MORTGAGES

The most basic advantage of an adjustable-rate mortgage (ARM) is that you benefit from lower interest rates when they are declining without having to go to the trouble and expense of refinancing, as you would have to do with a fixed-rate mortgage. If interest rates are high in relation to historic patterns, an ARM may be the more attractive option. But be careful about getting into the business of predicting interest rates. Even leading investment analysts and economists don't always accurately predict where rates are headed. Just because interest rates are high does not mean that they cannot go higher. That said, in times of inflation the ARM will be more attractive. Even on the downside, if interest rates do continue to rise, it is quite possible that your income will also rise, though probably not as fast.

It can be misleading to compare different ARMs strictly by interest rates. The initial interest rate on ARMs is often artificially low, what is called a teaser rate. This is a fine feature but dangerous if you are not prepared for a rate increase. Your mortgage will specify when the first adjustment will occur, which may be as soon as three months. For an accurate comparison of adjustable mortgages, use the true rate that, as described below, is tied to a specific index. Below are descriptions of other key features to consider when shopping for an ARM.

Caps.   A cap is the maximum amount the interest rate can rise on any one adjustment period or during the life of the loan. For example, a lender might quote a rate of 8 percent with a cap of 5 percent for the life of the loan and 1 percent per adjustment. You would know that the interest rate would never exceed 13 percent and would take at least five adjustment periods to reach that level. This feature adds a bit of predictability to an ARM and allows you to calculate the payments for worst-case scenarios. The combination of teaser rates and caps make ARMs an attractive option if you plan to stay in the house for a short period.

Adjustment periods.   ARMs come with different adjustment periods. Most lenders prefer an annual adjustment, but the periods do vary. What's best for the borrower is a low cap and a long adjustment period.

Payment caps.   In addition to capping the amount the interest rate can rise in one adjustment period, some mortgages cap the amount your payment can go up. For example, a loan with a 3/1 cap means that the interest rate could go up 3 percent each adjustment period, but the payment can only go up 1 percent. While this may seem to be a nice security, it could also lead to the dangerous situation of negative amortization. The amount of interest in excess of what is allowed by your payment cap will be added to the loan amount. So your loan will actually be getting bigger, not smaller, even though you continue to pay. Not good. Could become a mortgage bind, particularly if you're forced to sell at an inopportune time.

Indexes.   Your interest rate will be tied to an index. Your bank will add a margin, usually 2 to 5 percentage points, to the index of measurement. Common indexes are treasury securities, T-bills, the Federal Home Loan Bank Board (FHLBB) contract interest rate, and the 11th district cost of funds. You can research indexes in *The Wall Street Journal* or ask a lender. Try to come to an understanding of how rates fluctuate. Some, such as a 6-month T-bill, are quite volatile and therefore best to use when interest rates are very high. Others, such as 5-year treasury securities are very stable and would be best if interest rates are low. Of course, remember that the index is not your rate, and you must factor in the rate plus whatever the bank adds as a margin. The 5-year treasury securities index is usually only slightly lower than the prevailing fixed rate, so taking into account the margin, the price for this index's stability might be a less competitive interest rate.

And new twists to come.   It would be impossible to describe all the varieties of ARMs available, and new features will regularly crop up. One variation is a convertibility option that allows you to convert to a fixed rate after a period of time. This might be a good option if you'd really feel more comfortable with a fixed rate but need the easier qualification of an adjustable-rate mortgage. Once again, there is no replacement for shopping around to get a good picture of what's available.

■ FHA LOANS

The Federal Housing Administration insures lenders against default of FHA loans. Their backing allows the lenders to offer more liberal terms. The two main advantages of FHA loans are that your down payment requirements are lower than with conventional loans. The amount can fluctuate but has been about 3 percent to 5 percent. The second major advantage is that qualification ratios are more lenient, generally about 29 percent for housing debt and 41 percent for total debt.

FHA loans can be fixed or adjustable rates and come in a lot of varieties. It is essentially an insurance program, and the borrower pays the premium. There is an up-front mortgage insurance premium (MIP) charge that is fairly high (about 2 to 3 percent and subject to change), but it can be added to the loan amount. There is also an annual renewal premium, usually about ½ to 1 percent. In addition, the property must pass some fairly strict FHA inspections, all for your protection.

FHA loans can be a good option for a lot of middle-income buyers who are moderately qualified but who don't have much money for a down payment. The FHA sets maximum loan amounts that are based on property values in the area. You will be able to use these loans to buy houses priced at your area's median value or somewhat above.

■ VA LOANS

For those veterans who are eligible (you must have been on active duty during specified periods), the Department of Veterans Affairs (VA) loan program is a great entitlement, helping thousands of veterans get into reasonably priced homes. There is little or no down payment necessary, loan fees are modest and qualification criteria liberal. Interest rates are relatively low, and the VA determines the maximum interest rate the lender may charge and sets no limits on the amount of the loan. In effect, the maximum becomes the highest dollar amount of VA loan the secondary market is willing to purchase. The VA guarantees the loan, and the level of protection of borrower's rights in a default situation will be found nowhere else. The VA loans are assumable, even by nonveterans. That's the one way nonveterans can take advantage of the program.

As with the FHA loans, your property must pass an inspection. The application process will also take longer because of the bureaucracy. The first step is to obtain a Certificate of Eligibility from the Department of Veterans Affairs. Contact your closest VA office to find out if you qualify.

■ OTHER MORTGAGES

Here are the most common kinds of home mortgages used nowadays. Some may be available with a fixed-interest rate, others with an adjustable rate, and some with either fixed or adjustable rates. All are issued by private mortgage lenders. In other words, they fall under the generic heading of conventional mortgages.

The balloon mortgage. This is a good.option if you are certain that you will be in the home for a short period of time. The mortgage will carry a provision for a balloon payment to pay the full balance due at a defined period of time. The monthly payments prior to the end of the loan are based on a 30-year amortization schedule. Because the lender is essentially giving a short-term loan, balloon mortgages generally have attractive interest rates. Typical length of the loan would be five or seven years, or even three, though that would be more appropriate as a second mortgage. The downside is that if you are still in the home at the end of the term, you will have to come up with a substantial amount of money. If you don't have that kind of cash on hand, you'll have to refinance. There is always the risk that your financial situation would make qualification difficult or that you'll be forced to refinance in a period of high interest rates. You may have to sell the house.

The buydown mortgage. This is a financing technique that lowers the monthly payment during the early years of the mortgage. The buyer, seller, builder or other party pays a premium in the form of points that "buy down" or lower the interest rate for a set period of time.

The interest rate often stays low for two to five years, and then the rate goes up to the prevailing rate of mortgages. Compared with a higher-interest regular mortgage, the monthly payments for a buydown are lower, and a buydown can enable homebuyers to qualify for a larger mortgage and buy a higher-priced house.

The buydown was popular with builders in the early 1980s, so homebuyers could afford their houses despite the high interest rates of the time. The builder would subsidize the buydown mortgage in one way or another. The builder actually pays the mortgage lender the interest that is lopped off for the homebuyer. The price of the builder's houses may be increased to offset that expense, or part or all of the buydown cost may be absorbed. Sometimes the expense is offset in part or whole as a result of a business tax deduction.

In short, you may or may not be getting a free lunch when you get a buydown mortgage. One way to find out is by determining the sales prices for other new houses for sale nearby. If builders offering low-cost buydown mortgages are selling overpriced houses, they are not offering much of a bargain after all. Buydowns can also be offered by nearly anyone else selling a house, including the owners of used houses for sale.

The graduated payment mortgage.   This was developed to help young people buy houses that they otherwise couldn't afford. The monthly payments are reduced in the early years of the loan when a buyer's income is limited and higher payments might pose a burden. The payments increase periodically until they reach a fixed level, usually after five to ten years. Because the payments increase, a graduated payment mortgage (GPM) is suitable only for people who have good reason to believe that their income will increase. A GPM also costs somewhat more than a fixed-payment mortgage because part of the mortgage interest due is deferred in the early years when reduced payments are made. The unpaid interest is added to the principal to be paid off later and that can cause negative amortization. A GPM can often be obtained with either a fixed- or adjustable-interest rate but is risky nowadays, especially if there is any possibility you will be selling the property in a short period of time.

The shared-appreciation mortgage, or SAM.   A SAM allows anyone with money to invest in real estate to share the purchase of a house with a homebuyer who can't swing the deal alone. The investor, a friend, relative or anybody else chips in to pay a portion of the down payment, or of the monthly payments, or both. Both share ownership of the house and the income-tax deductions that can accrue.

The tax laws for this kind of mortgage can be complicated, so a good tax lawyer should be consulted. The buyer also may pay rent to the investor on the investor's portion of the property. A SAM is clearly for a buyer without the money needed to buy a house. It can also be for, among others, parents who wish to help children buy a house and to share the equity in the house.

Growing equity mortgage. This, a GEM (sic), calls for increased monthly mortgage payments each year for a specific number of years. It's for people with both the desire and the wherewithal to repay their mortgages more quickly than usual. The increase in payments goes to pay off the mortgage principal. In other words, it builds up equity in the house faster.

That's fine if you can swing it. But deliberately repaying a mortgage fast can mean less tax-deductible interest to be written off on annual income-tax returns. How important this is depends, of course, on your financial situation. And much the same growing-equity advantage can be obtained in almost any mortgage that stipulates no prepayment penalty, such as VA and FHA mortgages. But there the mortgage can be paid off at your own pace, and you're not tied down to a schedule. There may be no special advantage in a growing equity mortgage unless the lender offers you especially attractive mortgage terms, such as a significantly reduced interest rate, for example.

■ MORTGAGE TIPS

When shopping for a mortgage, remember that your search need not be limited to local mortgage lenders. Call other banks, mortgage bankers and credit unions. First, of course, try a bank or other lender with whom you do business for personal needs or through your company. That could entitle you to preferred treatment. But don't stop there. Try other lenders, including those in different parts of the country, as well as in your state and local area. Mortgage lenders and brokers, listed that way in the telephone classified pages, often can put you in touch with others elsewhere in the country who are looking for mortgage investments.

- Suppose you have difficulty dealing with a mortgage lender. If possible, discuss things with someone higher up, such as the vice president in charge of mortgages. He may have the authority to make concessions that those under him do not have.

- There are times when the home mortgage market turns into a buyer's market and the homebuyer is in the driver's seat. Then many a lender may want your business more than you need the lender. That's the result of an oversupply of mortgage money. Then you can often negotiate excellent concessions. Often, though, you must ask for them.

- Don't be cowed by bankers and don't be afraid to negotiate. "Too many people make the mistake of thinking that you may not bargain with a banker," says one expert. "They're awed by bankers." This shouldn't be. Much money is at stake.

- Most lenders no longer use prepayment penalty charges. If a mortgage lender insists on including a prepayment penalty charge in your mortgage, and you are committed to staying with the lender for other reasons, put a time limit on the charge. Prepayment penalties can be justified if a house is sold and the mortgage paid off within a year or two after the mortgage was issued. But the penalty should apply for no longer than five years at the most.

- Don't accept an acceleration clause in your mortgage. That permits a lender to demand and receive all of the money back; in other words, full repayment of the loan should you violate any one of a number of terms and restrictions, such as making an occasional late payment.

■ HOW TO FINANCE A HOUSE THAT YOU BUILD YOURSELF

When you buy a new or old house, it's usually a one-step financing operation. For more than 90 percent of all homebuyers, a home mortgage is obtained for the money to pay the seller, and the homebuyer repays it with monthly installments over a period of years.

No bank or any other mortgage lender, however, may legally issue a mortgage loan on an unfinished house, in other words, for a new house being built. Financing a house that you build yourself requires two-step financing. First comes an interim or construction loan that pays for the building materials and other expenses. Professional builders use construction loans all the time for building houses. The second step involves converting the construction loan into a house mortgage.

Naturally, there's an interest charge for construction money, and this can get expensive if you're not careful. The interest rate generally runs a few percentage points higher than the interest for home mortgage loans.

When you're ready to start building, however, don't just walk into your friendly neighborhood bank and ask for a construction loan. Do your homework first, especially because amateur or one-time homebuilders often start out with two strikes against them when they ask for construction money. Many bankers recoil at their request. They have a nightmare vision of getting stuck with a botched-up, unfinished house.

Apply as a professional would and you'll get a happy welcome. You should have the following three items: (1) a good land site for your house (it can help if you own the land and have already paid for it); (2) detailed plans and specifications for the house to be built; and (3) detailed cost estimates for the construction.

Mortgage lenders have varying requirements, so talk to a few in advance about what's needed. Things can be comparatively easy if your house is being built for you, from your plans, say, by a professional contractor. Financing may not be easily obtainable if you are serving as your own contractor and building your own house, at least in part with your own labor. Then you generally must prove that you have the skill and capability for such work. You also must have the wherewithal to repay the loan; in other words, a good job and regular income (or a rich aunt who will back you).

Building from a home manufacturer's house kit can simplify financing a house and also save you much time and money. A package with most or all the parts for the house, presized, measured and precut, is delivered, and you erect the house.

Some home manufacturers will finance the whole deal for you. If you own your land outright, it could provide the collateral for the down payment. Other manufacturers will steer you to a lender for financing. Most also provide the blueprints, cost estimates and other material needed to help you obtain the construction loan as well as a mortgage.

Speed of construction is one of the big advantages of building a factory house. It can sharply reduce the interest cost of your construction loan. For even a modest, no-frills house, the interest bill to finance the construction materials and other expenses can cost you up to $300 a month, if not more!

It often takes 12 to 18 months or more for a skilled do-it-yourselfer to build a house, while holding a full-time job. Thus interest costs can mount up—brace yourself—to literally thousands of dollars. That's where factory houses shine, because they can be completed in considerably less time. Hence a major savings can be realized on the money you borrow to finance construction.

Like a stick-built house that is built from scratch, when a factory house is completed, the construction loan is converted into a regular house mortgage.

■ ═══ CHAPTER 4 ═══ ■

The Vanishing Builder

There is no surer way to get stuck with a new house with small or big problems than to buy it from one of the vanishing-builder breed. The person may strike you as completely trustworthy, and indeed sometimes is—at least in the beginning. The house not only may be spanking new but may look as solidly constructed as any. It may even have passed the FHA or the VA inspection.

But when something goes wrong with it, the builder is no longer around. It may be a small thing—a warped door, sticky window, or leaky faucet—or it may be something really serious, such as chronic flooding of the basement, a defective furnace or a bum septic tank (and the plumbing backs up).

Whatever it is, your calls for help go unanswered, or you may find, to your surprise and distress, that there's no phone listing for the builder. In fact, there may never have been one. Builders simply may be unable or unwilling to make repairs. They may go out of business or leave town quietly. Whatever the reason, they have vanished as far as you are concerned. You are left high and dry (and sometimes not so dry).

Analyze all the instances in which homebuyers have been stuck with bad houses, and in nearly every one you'll find involved one form or another of the vanishing builder. The pattern becomes clear, and so does the obvious conclusion: There is no surer way of getting a good house than to avoid the vanishing builder. In short: Deal only with a reputable builder. That may smack of the stock advice offered freely and frequently by everyone who gives advice on homebuying. But it's easier said than done when you buy a house.

Before we get into how to avoid the vanishing-builder trap, be assured that the picture is not all dark. It should be emphatically said that by no means are most builders cheats, chiselers or con artists. We know of homebuilders with high principles who are Phi Beta Kappa graduates of Harvard and Yale. We personally know a good many with established records for building good houses. That kind of builder need not take a back seat to any business person in terms of professional ability, pride in craft, and quality of product.

There is also a gray area where builders, just like people in other professions and fields of business, sometimes skirt the edges of good ethics. Their houses may not be as honestly built and soundly constructed as top standards would call for, but they are not necessarily shoddy or jerry-built. There are also builders with honest intentions whose knowledge of construction and whose ability to perform unhappily fall short of those intentions.

Then there are the vanishing builders, the worst of the bunch. Spokespersons for the building industry contend that they make up a tiny minority of all builders, though the evidence suggests otherwise. Even if their number is not great, unfortunately their breed puts up a disproportionately large number of bad houses.

■ THE WAKE OF THE VANISHING BUILDER

A few examples should be cited together with a little detail about the vanishing builder. This can help you establish the profile of the kind of builder to avoid.

Item: A couple we'll call Johnson and ten other families bought houses with built-in time bombs in a place that we'll call Paradise Knolls. It's in a distant suburb of New York, a site of great natural beauty with the blue-gray Ramapo Mountains in resplendent view to the west.

After moving in, the Johnsons and their fellow neighbors had a series of troubles due to poor drainage. Their septic-tank systems constantly overflowed. "The sewage smell is awful," Mrs. Johnson told a reporter. She also said, "Water has seriously damaged our tile flooring, the wallboard is mildewing and water comes into the house so often we have all we can do to get rid of it. We brought in 32 truckloads of earth to divert the water . . . it only comes in more slowly. The State Supreme Court granted us a $3,000 judgment against the builder, but we can't collect."

Other families in Paradise Knolls must cope with sickening pools of smelly water in their basements, despite pumps going 24 hours a day to get rid of it. Pools of stagnant water overflow lawns and driveways. The embattled families tried for 18 months to get the builder to remedy their problems, but to no avail. The local Health Department is sympathetic but can do nothing. Other families also obtained court judgments against the builder but can't collect either.

The houses were built and sold by a builder from Long Island, another part of the state, who was apparently unable or unwilling to correct the problems. In effect, the builder has vanished (though is said to be building elsewhere under a different company name).

Item: A couple in a five-year-old home in suburban Fort Worth, Texas, has lived with walls that began cracking within months of their moving in. The builder had a Homeowners Warranty (HOW) insurance policy on the house. Originated by the National Association of Home Builders and later offered through an independent company, HOW is an insurance program that protects against major structural defects. Under legal obligation during the first two years to make repairs, the builder patched and painted and added 14 piers to the foundation. Then the interior of the house began to sag, and the builder added another 24 piers. The problems continued and, after the two-year period passed, the builder referred them to HOW, who sent engineers out to look at the problems. It took four months for the engineers to conclude that the foundation had been damaged. But HOW said the builder was responsible. The owners feel that they can never sell the house with all its cracks and bulges until the problems are solved. Now they are suing the builder and the warranty company.

The HOW program has undergone financial problems and is selling no new policies. There are other warranty policies available. Warranties give some recourse to buyers of new homes, but buyers shouldn't count on such warranties to make up for a shoddy or dishonest builder. The home warranties are designed to come through when the builder can't or won't pay. Most new home complaints are resolved directly with the builder. So the builder's willingness to make repairs is more important than any warranty the home carries. It is not unusual for builders and warranty companies to deflect liability toward one another, leaving the homebuyer in the lurch. That is one type of vanishing act. The builder who is indifferent to customers is not much better than a builder who skips town altogether.

Item: A slew of roof-leak problems arising from use of a fire-retardant (FRT) plywood illustrates the range of builder responses to a bad situation. The plywood was used on townhouses and condominiums in 35 states east of the Mississippi during the 1980s. Designed to slow the spread of flames to adjoining homes, the FRT plywood was unfortunately prone to deterioration. Homebuilders blamed the chemicals used in treating the plywood. The plywood industry, defending its product, claimed the problem was caused by high moisture levels in some homes due to poor ventilation and improper construction techniques. The cost to repair all the defective roofs was estimated at $2 billion.

Tens of thousands of homes in the Washington, D.C. area were affected. According to the *Washington Post*, several large homebuilders said they would pay to repair or replace deteriorating roofs and filed suit against the plywood treaters, suppliers and other companies to recoup their costs. Not everyone was so fortunate. One builder instructed homeowners to seek compensation from the manufacturers and suppliers of the treated plywood. In its defense, the company argued that using the FRT plywood was in compliance with building codes, and the makers of the plywood should be responsible. Another company notified hundreds of townhouse owners that it had used the treated plywood but offered no remedy for problems. A few months later that company filed for Chapter 11 bankruptcy protection.

The problem affected entire developments. Owners of units who had bought from builders who refused to make the repairs organized class action suits. One resident claimed that a survey of the 174 townhouses in her development showed that 172 had roof leaks. Whatever the real cause of the leaking roofs, both good builders and not-so-good builders suffered from it. The good builders took care of their customers first and then went after the plywood suppliers.

■ HOW DO SUCH THINGS HAPPEN?

How does the vanishing builder get away with it? And doesn't the homebuyer have any recourse?

One of the biggest culprits is the floating vanishing builder, who generally operates in a large metropolitan area. Sometimes the "floater" hastily puts together a building operation staked by investors who latch on to a chunk of land in order to make a killing in housing. They often know little or nothing about house construction. Often they're not even builders. They just have some land and some capital and a burning desire to make a quick profit.

Such firms generally care little about the quality of the houses being put up. They aim for fast construction and even faster sales. When the last house is finished and sold, the profits are divided up and the corporation is disbanded. If anything goes wrong with the houses, the "builder" can easily duck responsibility even if the homeowners haul the builder into court.

The *Fresno Bee* reported that in Northern California 30 homeowners sued Sunland Communities of Northern California, Inc., for breach of contract after what they said was two years of reporting many problems that never were repaired, including malfunctioning heat and air-conditioning systems; poor paint quality; leaking roofs, windows, and pipes; cracked tiles; the use of substandard materials; and structural deformities. After losing a $4.4 million lawsuit, the chief executive officer announced in a letter to the homeowners who hadn't sued that the cost of the judgment and fighting the suit had exhausted all money set aside to make repairs. He advised the homeowners to pursue repairs through subcontractors and insurance companies. Sunland's license expired, and the chief executive officer said the company was out of funds and out of business, though he had not declared bankruptcy. Meanwhile he held licenses for two other building companies operating in San Diego, that, he explained, were under different ownership and had nothing to do with Sunland Communities of Northern California.

That should alert you to the first ominous portent of potential trouble. When houses in a new development are being put up by builders with a new corporation, often the corporation has been formed just to develop a single group of houses. Be on guard even if the builders proudly tell you about other houses they have built; you may find that they were built under other corporate names.

An established professional builder doesn't form new corporations all the time but rather sticks with one company name. This is not necessarily to say that every new corporation putting up houses should be suspected. You can't necessarily tell for sure. But because it is a major identifying mark of the vanishing builder, the new corporation builder should be viewed with a strong dose of skepticism. It could be your first clue that all is not right.

The vanishing builder usually has little or no fear of the law. The law, in fact, has by and large proved ineffectual with such builders. That includes most district attorneys, other public officials or agencies (such as your attorney general), the FHA, the VA, and anybody else you might think could help. All of these people are by law concerned only with criminal violations. To nail a recalcitrant builder, they need clear evidence of fraud. This is often tough to get, or so they say. As a result, the typical district attorney may listen to your woes sympathetically but in the end give you the brush-off. We're dreadfully sorry, the district attorney will say, but it's so darned hard to prove fraud. Patting you on the back in consolation, while leading you to the door, the district attorney will say that you'll have to hire a lawyer and take the case to civil court.

It is because of the glaring indifference shown by many law enforcement people that some builders have continued to build inferior houses. If officials would get tough, there would be far fewer abuses in home construction.

Some time ago, an atypical district attorney led a crackdown on builders stemming from complaints in an outlying Brooklyn area. After nearly three years of investigation, the district attorney convicted one builder of first-degree grand larceny. Though the conviction was later overturned in a higher court, the case made it clear to other builders that the district attorney meant business. Five other builders were indicted. A city plumbing inspector was convicted of taking bribes. Eight FHA inspectors and a VA construction official were also indicted on bribery charges brought by the federal government. An Assistant District Attorney noted, "Shoddy construction goes hand-in-hand with corrupt inspectors." The most significant outgrowth of the case was its effect on other builders. The chief of the Brooklyn Rackets Bureau said, "After our indictment, it was amazing how fast builders made repairs."

What help can you expect if something goes wrong with a house you buy with an FHA or VA mortgage? Both agencies inspect homes before approving loans and will put pressure on the builder to correct defects that show up during the first year of ownership, the period covered by the usual warranty. This often produces results, because builders not following through will be, in effect, blacklisted by both agencies and will no longer be allowed to build and sell houses with VA or FHA mortgages. But the government can't force builders to make repairs. Some builders refuse, apparently unconcerned about a government blacklisting. They can still build and sell houses with conventional mortgages.

■ OTHER REASONS FOR PROBLEM BUILDERS

Building houses is an exceedingly tough business. It holds pitfalls for builders as well as for buyers. This brings on hardships that are sometimes beyond the builder's ability to cope with. Some builders are betrayed by chiseling subcontractors or by callous workers who mess up a house and cover up the shoddy work. There is also the time-consuming difficulty of finding good subcontractors and then getting them to show up at the proper time. Many builders also face an incredible hodgepodge of local regulations and arbitrary building code demands, making it impossible to build efficiently. And then there are the exasperating obstacles put in the builder's path by some political bureaucrats who run things with dictatorial hands from power posts in municipal building departments. That includes some building inspectors whose performance leaves much to be desired, as well as those who reportedly shake down builders.

As a result of such difficulties, the builder's lot is not easy. Hard-pressed builders can find themselves in quite a jam, much of it not their own doing. No wonder then that some will throw up their hands in despair, saying there must be an easier way to make a living, and pull out, leaving their homebuyers holding the bag. We mention that side of the coin not only in fairness to those builders who strive hard to satisfy, but also to give a more rounded picture of the industry. Don't blame the builders for everything that goes wrong.

The builder's sales agents you encounter in a model house also rate a few words, because they can do you in (and also your builder). No matter how good the builders, one of their salespersons can mislead you. Good salespeople are hard to come by. Even the best builders have little control over the wild promises and misstatements of some salespeople. They may be quick to tell you what a short distance it will be to the new soon-to-be-built school or reassure you that the streets will be paved by a certain date. That's fine if such information is true. If it is vital information for you, though, it had better be double-checked.

■ THE HALLMARKS OF THE GOOD BUILDER

How do you tell if builders are really good and reliable? Can you count on them to make amends if something goes wrong in a house they built? In short, should you buy a house from these builders?

The kind of builder you're dealing with can be determined in much the same way that you check on other people you will have serious dealings with, including doctors and lawyers. What is the builder's reputation? What about the builder's track record? Ask others who have bought from the builder, says a spokesperson for the National Association of Home Builders. That's old advice, to be sure, but it can be forever revealing.

There are also a few special characteristics, or hallmarks, that are generally common among the better builders. A firm might gain acclaim for, among other things, their excellent community planning, technological innovation or an unusual number of special features while keeping prices competitive. There are a couple other important hallmarks of a top-notch builder. Look for builders who have been in business with one company (no corporation folding) and use their family name. That's not to say that there are not reputable builders who don't meet these criteria, but you should be skeptical. Even among the largest builders in the country—billion dollar companies—you'll see family names, such as Ryland Group, Kauffman and Broad Home Corp., or Pulte Corp.

■ HOW TO CHECK ON A BUILDER

Most, though not necessarily all, reputable builders use their own names as part of their firm name. The builder's advertising, the signs around the houses, and the promotion material should play up the family name.

Be wary, on the other hand, of the builders who promote a particular tract name such as Happy Knolls or Sunshine Acres, with little or no emphasis on their name. Those builders are ones who should make you cautious. It could be the first sign of a vanishing builder.

Here is a checklist of other pointers for avoiding the vanishing builder and getting a good house.

❑ *Has the builder been established in business for some time?*

The longer the builder has operated under the same name, the longer you can expect that the company will be around in the future to take care of possible problems. By and large, the well-established builder also has a permanent office headquarters in the area. Some builders live in one of their own houses nearby, perhaps the greatest accolade one could ask for. Building is for them a lifetime profession.

Check on these things by obtaining a financial report on the builder. It can usually be had for a few dollars through your local bank. The report will also give an indication of the builder's credit rating. A low rating is clearly not good. Also ask the builder for credit references, including banks. Check with each one. How long has the builder been in business? How reliable is the builder?

□ *Does the builder have a record of building good houses?*

Good builders will often have pictures of their houses on the office walls. Ask where you can see houses they have built and ask for the names of at least half a dozen past buyers. See or call them; this is one of the best ways to find out how you are likely to fare.

□ *Do local building material suppliers and subcontractors give the builder a good rating?*

Talk to the builder's lumber dealer, plumbing supplier, and others, as well as people in the local building department. These people know which builders cause trouble and which do not, though sometimes they are reluctant to criticize. If no one can say much good about a builder, beware.

□ *Is the builder a member of the local chapter of the National Association of Home Builders?*

If so, it's a decided plus factor. Call the local association to find out. It's usually listed in the telephone book under "Home Builders" or "Associations." If a member, the builder is among the better, if not the best, builders in the area.

To be sure, not every member of the builders association may deserve a high ranking, any more than every member of the American Bar Association is a top lawyer. But if a serious problem arises with a builder who is a member, the association can, if necessary, put pressure on the builder to take remedial action.

□ *Call the Better Business Bureau about your builder.*

If it can report nothing, it means no complaints have been received. Of course, this may not mean anything. If they report one or more complaints on the builder's record, the complaints should have been addressed. If not, it's a danger signal.

☐ *Does the builder have a listed telephone number?*

It should not be a new number under the name of the development, such as for "Good Ole Rolling Acres" or "Sunset by the Sea." It should be in the name of the builder or the established firm. If not, watch out. Besides, if there's no permanent telephone listing, whom do you call with a problem after you buy the house?

A builder who scored high on the checklist is the very best assurance of your getting a well-built house. You can almost forget about peering into dark corners, checking the two-by-fours, and knocking on walls to see if they are solid. The house should be fairly well constructed at the very least. A good builder doesn't want call-backs or trouble any more than you do. They cost money and time that eats into profit. But if something in the house doesn't work right, the odds are high that the good builder will take care of it. You will have little to worry about.

Conversely, you should look again, carefully, at the houses of a builder who scores low on the checklist. This is the stage at which to tread slowly, even though houses seem well built when you inspect them. It's because—and let's face it—most of us know little more about the intricacies of house construction than we know about laser beams. (And even if you happen to know about lasers, it doesn't make you a house construction expert.) Check out the builder first, rather than the construction of the builder's houses, and you've made probably the biggest possible step forward toward getting a well-built house.

■ ══ CHAPTER 5 ══ ■

The No-Design House

The no-design house lacks style, proportion and beauty. But that's not all. There's more to design, or the lack of it, than mere good looks.

The no-design house is hard to live in and a nightmare to cope with and maintain. It's stuck on its lot with no thought given to taking advantage of the best view or the best exposure in relation to the overhead sun or the prevailing winds (heat and cold). Little or no thought is given to the occupants' privacy from passing traffic out front or from the eyes of neighbors on either side. And inside, the interior plan and room arrangements are often just as bad for meeting the needs of the people who will live here.

That brings up the three main ingredients of a well-designed house: (1) good appearance, (2) a well-planned house-to-site relationship, and (3) good interior planning. The only way to avoid the no-design house and get a house you will enjoy thoroughly and that will retain its resale value and be really satisfactory over the years is to understand these three essentials of good design and how to spot them when you shop for a house. We shall discuss the first two points here and the third in Chapter 6.

■ GOOD APPEARANCE

Take a good look at a no-design house: You will often find that the facade is likely to be broken up with a mish-mash of different materials put together like a banana split.

It may include blotches of stone or brick mixed in with two or three different kinds of wood siding. There is no coherence. You'll generally see walls jutting in or out here and there with many jogs and breaks. The roof lines are often broken up for no reason at all. This is supposed to add variety and interest but creates visual chaos instead. The doors and windows not only do not line up, but are often out of scale and character with the rest of the house. And here and there is hideous gingerbread adding to the clutter, like cheap jewelry piled over a flashy dress.

What is good appearance? One of the best answers was given in a book for professionals, now out of print, *Construction Lending Guide: A Handbook of Homebuilding Design and Construction*, written by architects John L. Schmidt, Walter H. Lewis, and Harold Bennett Olin, for the United States Savings and Loan League. Here are some things the book has to say about good appearance.

Exterior Appearance

Pleasing appearance is no accident. Careful study and organization are necessary to anticipate how a house will appear in finished form. The appreciation of a well-designed building is based on recognition and evaluation of the following points.

Proper Proportions

There are basic combinations of shape and mass that result in balanced building proportions. Portions of a building can be out of balance, just as a scale can be tilted. In traditional styling, the proportions of structures and the elements within the design have been refined through many years of study. Roof slopes, overhangs, window shapes, and sizes have all been carefully considered to fit with one another. In today's typical house design (in attempting to achieve the charm of traditional styling) familiar elements are often used without exercising proper care for achieving pleasing proportions.

Visual Organization

A house is a complex arrangement of parts and pieces. Success in exterior design rests in large part on the visual continuity of these elements, which should be related in shape, form and arrangement. Visual organization is the assembling of the parts and pieces with these relationships in mind.

Material Usage, Textures

Materials should be selected for uses appropriate to their capabilities. The elements of a house should be built of materials capable of performing satisfactorily, both initially and over the years.

The visual response aroused by various materials differs greatly. For example, the smooth, "cold" flatness of porcelain-enamel steel panels affects a viewer very differently from a rough, nubby stone wall of rich "warmth." The texture of materials is extremely important in the design of houses and in the selection of materials to be used.

In general, the number of textures selected should be held to a minimum—one type of masonry, one type of wood, or one siding texture, and one neutral "panel" surface per house. Contrasts can be used very successfully, just as a man can be well-dressed with a coat and trousers of different texture. The well-dressed man, however, and the well-dressed house do not wear many varying materials at the same time.

Scale

Scale is the relationship of design elements to the human being. One's visual sense depends in great part on scale relationships in judging distances, sizes and proportions. The size of a door in a house facade can be "in scale," that is, proportioned agreeably to the human being and to the rest of the house; or it can be "out of scale," that is, not properly related to the human figure, overpowering or diminutive in the entire design.

Simplicity and Restraint

To simplify is to refine. In housing, the simplest, most basic designs are the hardest to achieve but simple visual elements are the most pleasing. The attempt to make a house appear more expensive by cheap imitation of expensive items can be disastrous.

Scrollwork and carpentry bric-a-brac can result in design chaos. Such an approach is often based on using many unrelated elements in an effort to develop curb appeal. A storm door with a pelican scroll, a checkerboard garage door, slanted posts at the entranceway, diamond-shaped windows and other parts and pieces having no design continuity detract from appearance and result in a modest house looking cheaper instead of costlier.

The most successful approach is one of restraint. Generally, the simply stated house design is the handsomest. Restraint and sophistication go hand in hand. And opulence and over-decoration are more often than not annoying and disturbing. The simplest designs are the most agreeable in the long run.

Color

Color is a highly potent factor in the design of a group of houses taken as a whole. In this respect, color coordination is a major way to strengthen that pleasing individuality from house to house, the objective of good subdivision design. Color is actually so powerful that it can make a cracker-box house look attractive or a generally well-designed house look repulsive. It all depends on the skill with which color is used. When a large group of houses is involved, the overall effect of color is a major concern. The cluttered, disorganized look of the average subdivision of low-to-moderate-priced houses (or even more expensive ones) is due largely to lack of color coordination. Clashing roofs, anemic body colors, misplaced accent colors—all these result from the short-sighted practice of giving the buyer too much latitude in selecting exterior color.

The All-Round Look

Unfortunately, most houses are designed like a Hollywood set. Some concern is evidenced over the appearance of the street facade, but often the side and rear elevations are totally neglected. A well-designed house, like a piece of sculpture, should be handsome when viewed from any vantage point.

A Few Words about Style

A well-known architect, Alden Dow, FAIA, puts it simply: "Style is a result, it can never be an objective. When style itself becomes the objective, nothing results but a copy."

What determines style? The shape and character, or style, of a house should be determined by the plan, the site, methods and materials of construction, and by the budget. A particular set of circumstances, worked upon by the design process, logically will lead to a particular set of building shapes or appearance. It might be correct to say that the well-designed house is styleless, since no forcing of the solution has been made by adapting it to the framework of a "traditional" scheme. Traditional styles are, of course, in predominance and undoubtedly will remain so for many years. But there are other styles to consider.

Here are four terms often discussed in describing other than traditional architecture: modern, modernistic, contemporary, and futuristic.

A *modern* house is one built of up-to-date materials: it has most of the current electrical and mechanical gadgetry in place and may exhibit itself as a simplified expression of any of the whole bag of traditional styles. It is harmless in design—not bad perhaps—but not great architecture.

A *modernistic* house is a poorly designed, "jazzy" modern house. Often it is an attempt at being unusual, generally is designed by a contractor or individual and is usually a collection of pieces (perhaps a flat roof or a butterfly roof, round windows, slanted posts, big "picture windows") with no integration of parts into a carefully studied design.

A *contemporary* house generally is one done by an architect and grows in its design from the consideration of beauty, function, and site. The market confuses good contemporary design with modernistic and fails to perceive the great difference between the two. Contemporary design is not faddish, or subject to being "in" today, "out" tomorrow. On the contrary, it's extremely rare, especially in lower-cost houses.

A *futuristic* house is somewhat experimental in nature. New products or methods may be tried or tested, and generally the futuristic house attempts to present an image of tomorrow's house. It may be, and usually is, a properly conceived design, but its importance on the market is inconsequential.

Poorly designed modernistic houses invariably will be penalized by the market, but an honestly conceived contemporary home, large or small, is of lasting value. Little research is necessary to recognize that a fine piece of architecture appreciates in value and appeal. Certainly the demand far exceeds the small supply.

■ ARCHITECTURAL STYLES

A few additional words should be said about the sensitive subject of "style." What architectural style is for you? You may prefer a traditional style, such as a Cape Cod or English Colonial house, or your taste may swing to the present in favor of an up-to-date contemporary house. Whatever you like, it's your prerogative. Stick to your guns.

However, words like "Colonial" and "contemporary" stir up fierce emotions, and one's sensitivities are easy to wound. Let's avoid that sort of thing and understand some of the basic facts and reasons surrounding the main kinds of American houses and how their designs developed. A look back can be instructive.

The Cape Cod House

Consider the Cape Cod house, a remarkable structure for its time and place (see Figure 5.1). It was originally a tight little box with a massive chimney set in the dead center of the house. The chimney anchored the house against the shifting sands and howling winds of Cape Cod. The chimney was flanked by a small room on each side of the front door and in the rear by a large kitchen. That let each room of the house have its own fireplace built into the central chimney. The rooms were small because a fireplace could not heat much space.

The windows were small and shuttered (storm sash) to keep out windblown sand as well as the fierce winds of winter. The windows consisted of numerous small panes (lites) because the glassblowing methods of the time could not turn out large panes. The house usually faced square to the south—not only to receive a maximum of warm sunshine in winter, but also to tell time. When the sun's rays came straight in a front window, hitting the marker on the floor, it was high noon.

It was the thriftiest sort of house, low and broad of beam, and measuring 38 feet by 29 feet, with ceilings only 7 feet high. The extra half-floor in the attic was originally left open as a dormitory. Straw pallets or trundle beds were put down for any number of children. As the family expanded—and some had as many as 26 offspring, according to old diaries—lean-tos were built on the side or back to sleep the overflow. The houses were never expanded upward. The large kitchen at the back, with its huge fireplace and built-in brick oven, was the natural center of activity for the family. In the summer, though, its stifling

FIGURE 5.1 ■

The Jabez Wilder House, South Massachusetts, was built about 1690. It is the kind of Cape Cod house with a bow roof, curved like the keel of a ship, built by a people familiar with shipbuilding techniques. The main house is almost as deep as it is wide; note how it hugs the ground. (*Charles Peterson, HABS, Library of Congress*)

heat was too much, and a separate summer kitchen was often added at the back.

Over the years the basic design of the Cape Cod was changed and varied, and later it lost favor as Americans turned to other styles. But then later, much later, the Cape Cod reemerged as a popular house during the Depression days of the 1930s. Casting around for a thrifty and compact house to put up and sell, homebuilders resurrected the Cape Cod, though not without serious modifications and changes not all to the good. That's why today you will see thousands upon thousands of Cape Cods of one kind or another along the highways and byways of our country. They kept on building them following World War II, though by this time the fundamental reasons for an authentic or even modified Cape Cod were no longer valid.

FIGURE 5.2 ■

The handsome, unadorned design of the Parson Capen House in Topsfield, Massachusetts, still stands out, though it was built in 1683. Wayne Andrews has called it "probably the finest remaining example of seventeenth-century American domestic architecture." (*Photo: Wayne Andrews*)

The Colonial and Later Houses

In the early days the Cape Cod was followed by five basic kinds of colonial houses: the English, French, Dutch, Spanish, and Southern Colonial. The early settlers tried to build houses that were as nearly as possible like their former homes in Europe but were forced to adapt them to a new climate, new materials, and different building conditions (see Figure 5.2). The Southern colonists from England did better than their New England relatives, thanks to a milder climate and the availability of bricks and slave labor. They were better able to reflect the Georgian style (see Figure 5.3) of eighteenth-century England (as in Williamsburg, Virginia). The classical revival in England

FIGURE 5.3 ■

The George Wythe House in Williamsburg, Virginia, built with native brick, is called a perfect example of Georgian Colonial architecture. It was built in 1755 for Wythe, the first professor of law at William and Mary College. (*Colonial Williamsburg*)

was later copied in the Southern plantation mansions with their two-story columns. The French settlers along the St. Lawrence River did not do well because of the lack of suitable materials. The French in New Orleans fared better, partly because the best architects were sent to Louisiana.

The New Amsterdam Dutch did splendidly, coming closest to duplicating their Holland dwellings, as testified by the fine old Dutch Colonials still standing along the Hudson River valley. The Spanish influence was short-lived in Florida but eventually survived in the Southwest, where it was well carried out with adobe, plaster and other available materials.

In the nineteenth century the Gothic revival in England swept over to influence American architecture, and we had our hands full with Victorian houses of every kind and shape.

Then came the ranch house, an indigenous design, springing up from the sprawling ranch houses of the West. They were suitable for people who could afford a large house spread out luxuriously on cheap land. The ranch reached its acme of excellence in the prairie houses of Frank Lloyd Wright (see Figure 5.4 and Figure 5.5). Today we also have the Bauhaus school of modern architecture, illustrated at its best by exciting glass houses stemming from the work of architects Ludwig Mies van der Rohe and Philip Johnson. Some of their imitators, however, have cursed us with monstrous botched-up glass houses.

The Modern House

A good modern house makes plenty of sense today, largely because of central heating, a key influence on twentieth-century architecture. It lets us enjoy big rooms with large windows without discomfort. There's no longer any need for a fireplace in every room. With no longer a need for a coal bin, a basement is not essential (though it can be great for storage and utility purposes). And because of air-conditioning, every room no longer requires two exposures for cross-ventilation.

In short, new materials and modern techniques can make a huge difference in the way houses are designed and built today, in contrast with the way houses were traditionally designed (and styled) in the past. For example, today, by using triple-glaze, we can use large areas of glass, thus opening our houses to sun, light and view without letting in cold and drafts.

That's the case, somewhat oversimplified to be sure, for a good contemporary house design. You may still prefer a traditional house, assuming it gives you modern living advantages. But another characteristic of house design should be considered: the number of floor levels.

FIGURE 5.4 ■

Frank Lloyd Wright's Robie House, built in Chicago in 1908, ranks as one of the most significant American houses of the twentieth century. It broke with the past and led the way to contemporary architecture in houses. (*Photo: Wayne Andrews*)

■ HOW MANY FLOOR LEVELS?

There are one-story, one-and-a-half-story, two-story, and split-level houses. The one you choose can have an enormous influence on your day-to-day living convenience and pleasure. Knowing the pros and cons of each can also help you single out the best type for your family.

The One-Story House

The one-story house (ranch or bungalow) excels for its glorious lack of stair climbing, a boon for the parents of small children as well as for elderly people. It's suitable for people with low, medium or high incomes. It's the easiest kind of house to keep clean and maintain. This means not only reduced housekeeping labor and chores but also reduced maintenance and upkeep expenses. For example, it has been estimated that the cost of painting the inside and

FIGURE 5.5 ∎

Falling Water, designed by Frank Lloyd Wright, was built in 1936 for E. J. Kaufmann, Bear Run, Pennsylvania. (*Photo: Wayne Andrews*)

outside of a one-story house runs 15 percent to 23 percent-less than the cost of painting a two-story house. (One of the reasons is the higher ladder cost for a two-story house.)

The one-story house allows the most flexible floor planning. It opens up the advantages of indoor-outdoor living (that much-used magazine phrase) to people in every room. Though it works best on flat land, it can be built on any terrain. Wherever it's built, though, it should hug the ground for aesthetic reasons and for safety. A one-story house looks awkward and ungainly when it sticks way up out of the ground and when extra steps from the house to ground level are required. The fewer the steps, the better, particularly at night, when it's hard to see and accidents are more likely.

The main drawbacks of the one-story house have to do with its room zoning and construction. Because all rooms are side-by-side on one level, good separation between the living, working and sleeping zones is essential. The spread-out plan also requires more land, making it usually more expensive, and the one-story house requires more roof and basement area than a multilevel house with the same overall interior space (though it's not so costly as you may think).

The One-and-a-Half-Story House

Fewer and fewer Cape Cods, the classic one-and-a-half-story American house, are built these days because of the difficulty and expense of turning that raw unfinished attic into usable rooms. A full two-story house generally costs no more and usually less. Besides, the attic rooms in a Cape Cod, being under the roof, tend to be furnace-hot in summer and icy cold in winter. Special care in insulation and heating is essential to prevent these problems; but it is not always provided.

Dormer windows in the roof can violate the basic lines of the authentic Cape Cod and spoil the looks. If there's a basement under the house, the hole necessary for the stair-well can wreak havoc with the compact first-floor plan, where every square foot counts. In fact, recent research has shown that because of the space lost to the stairways up and down, plus such things as the extra materials required for the steep roof, the Cape Cod is one of the costliest houses to build in terms of the net living space you get. So, sad to say, the charming old Cape Cod takes a backseat today to other, more economical and convenient kinds of houses.

The Two-Story House

A two-story house gives a feeling of large size and permanence and comes closest to our blurred notions of "Colonial." It leads the field in getting the most house on the least land. It's therefore supremely feasible on high-priced land or on a tight little lot. It offers natural separation (zoning) between the living activities downstairs and the bedrooms upstairs. It's also for people who have qualms about sleeping in bedrooms at ground level. Because it's compact, it can be somewhat easier to heat than a house on one spread-out floor level. And in summer the downstairs rooms tend to be cool, though the upstairs bedrooms can get quite hot if the attic isn't properly insulated and ventilated.

Its main drawback is the stair climbing, which makes house-cleaning tougher and puts great strain on parents of small children and on the elderly. It also puts restrictions on a family that likes to spend a lot of time outdoors, during nice weather. Though the downstairs can be designed for easy access to outdoors, it's amazing how often you must come in and trudge up and down the stairs when you're doing things outdoors.

Ordinarily the two-story house should cost less to build than any other house, but not as much less as you might think. Extra room area must be provided to compensate for the space lost to the upstairs stairway, and what is saved on roofing area is partly if not entirely canceled out by the expense of getting materials to the second floor and roof.

The Split-Level House

The split-level is the house for a sloping lot; you can have at least two main floors with direct access to outdoors. There are side-to-side splits and front-to-back ones, depending on the slope and the best way to face the house (i.e., it can be built well on any slope). The different parts of the house can be zoned off from each other by putting them on different levels. Properly designed, a good split can look handsome and large, with the additional advantage of only a short stairway from one level to another.

Improperly designed, a split with numerous, short stairways can be a decided pain in the neck (and legs). You find yourself going up and down far too often. The split is also complex, if not difficult, to build. This can run up its cost, especially if excessive bulldozing and grading are necessary or if retaining walls must be built. The lowest and highest levels demand especially good heating and insulation for comfort. The worst split-level houses—the no-design kind—are those that are stuck on a dead-level lot. That can make them look ungainly and awkward because they are unsuitable for a flat lot. The best ones, built on sloping land, look as if they grew out of a natural marriage between land and house.

Which Way Should Your House Face?

The placement of a house on its lot is the second vital ingredient of design. Ideally, the main living areas and the main windows should drink in the best view and should also face south. The best view isn't always to the south, but we'll get to that in a moment. You can quickly tell if you will enjoy the best view simply by looking out the windows when you inspect a house. Is it a good vista? It may be a simple, serene view of grass and trees or a panoramic view of the Rocky Mountains or the Pacific Ocean. Or all you may see is asphalt street or a view of your neighbor's clothesline. A clothesline view is, of course, another mark of the no-design house.

The accompanying sun diagram in Figure 5.6 shows why a southern exposure is ordinarily best: because of the predictable course changes of the overhead sun from season to season. In summer it rises in the northeast at morning and sets in the northwest. In winter, however, you'll see how the morning sun rises in the southeast, arcs across the sky at a much lower, more southerly direction, and sets in the southwest.

A southern exposure is therefore the only exposure that can let bright, warm sunshine flood into your house all winter long. This means not only that your house will be bright and delightfully pleasant with sunshine, but that your fuel bills may be lower. A southern exposure can also pay off in a cooler house in summer, because windows on the south are easy to shade from the hot sun—with deciduous shade

FIGURE 5.6 ■

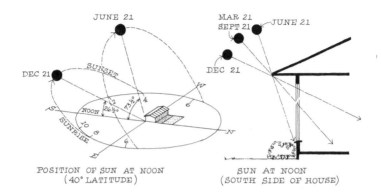

POSITION OF SUN AT NOON
(40° LATITUDE)

SUN AT NOON
(SOUTH SIDE OF HOUSE)

This illustration shows how the orbit of the overhead sun varies over the United States from the longest day in summer to the shortest day in winter. It also shows how a roof overhang on the south side of a house can shade a big window from hot sun in summer but let warm sunshine in the same window in winter. (*All About Houses*)

trees that obligingly lose their leaves in winter to let the sunshine through, or by deep roof over-hangings that block out the overhead summer sun but let in the lower-angled southern sun in winter.

As for other exposures, a house that faces east or west gets the fierce brunt of hot sun in either the morning or the afternoon in summer (when you certainly don't want it) but much less sun during those cold days of winter. A house that faces north not only gets little sunshine in winter, but must bear the full bitter lash of cold winds in winter.

Sun versus View

Naturally the best view isn't always to the south. If it is not, a compromise is in order. A good middle ground is not impossible. Some big windows can be located to receive the view, whereas others face south to receive the winter sun. If you are buying a development house, ordinarily you have a choice of lots, so you can choose one that combines the best

FIGURE 5.7 ■

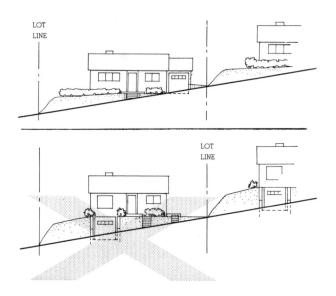

Right way to site a house on a sloping street (top) puts garage on same level, reducing steps and driveway slope as well as excavation cost. Wrong way (below) shows awkwardness that results when the opposite is done. (*All About Houses*)

view with a southern exposure. You can also ask for design changes, if necessary, so the house is sited on its lot for the best orientation in relation to sun and view.

The House/Site Design

The house should be sited to give you the most use from your land. Mentally divide the lot into its three main areas: the public, the private and the service zones. The public zone consists of the front lawn and that part of the grounds in public view. The private zone embraces that part, usually on the sides and/or rear of the house, reserved for your private outdoor use. The service zone includes the driveway, the walks, and the areas for trash cans, outdoor-equipment

FIGURE 5.8 ■

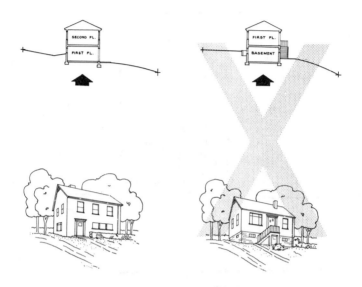

Right way to site a house on sloping lot (left) puts first floor at ground level. Wrong way (right) raises house awkwardly above ground, making it look out of joint as well as adding extra steps. (*All About Houses*)

storage, and other such needs. Figure 5.9 illustrates placement of the house on the lot.

Ideally, a house should be set forward on its lot to give you the most amount of your land for private use in the rear, out of sight of neighbors and passing traffic. That also means a minimum of public zone in the front and thus minimal need for lawn-mowing and landscaping. You cut down on maintenance chores, leaving yourself more time to be out back, either at play with children or simply relaxing with a drink in your hand on your patio or terrace. Such outdoor living space can be easily created when the house is properly located on its lot. It may require help in the form of fences to screen the private part of your land from the view of outsiders.

FIGURE 5.9 ■

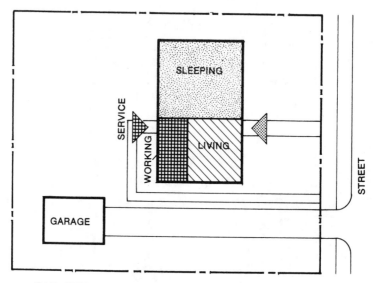

OLD WAY TO PLACE HOUSE ON INSIDE LOT

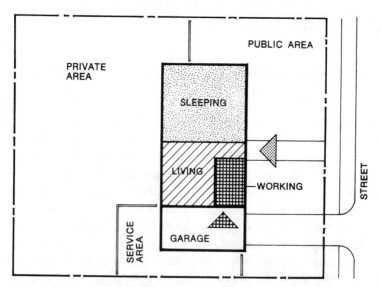

GOOD HOUSE PLACEMENT AND LAYOUT FOR INSIDE LOT

FIGURE 5.10 ■

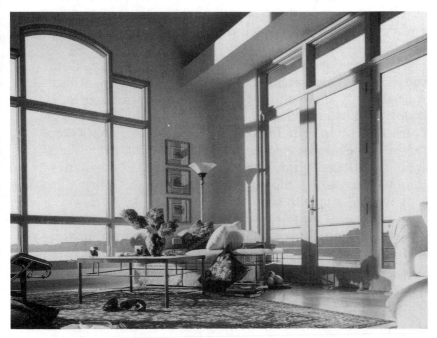

This lakefront house was designed to provide maximum living pleasure from a fine indoor-outdoor relationship. Liberal use of glass helps warm the house while admitting light and offering views at every turn. The result is a feeling of great spaciousness. But be forewarned, even with air-conditioning, large glass areas like this demand careful planning, orientation and shading from hot sun. (*Photo courtesy of Andersen Windows, Inc.*)

The private zone of the lot should also have a good connection to the living zones of the house itself. The living areas inside the house should be located with convenient access to the patio or terrace, and vice versa. More on this in the next chapter, where we take up the third vital ingredient of good design—interior planning.

To sum up the no-design house, it can usually be spotted within moments after you get out of your car to inspect a house. Is there too much lawn to mow and maintain in front, too little land for private, low-upkeep use in the back? Take a look at the overhead sun. How much of it gets into the house during cold weather? How much is kept out during warm weather? Does the house capture the best view? These are some of the functional things that you can measure by eye. And, of course, what about the overall style and design? Is it really well designed, or is it a no-design house?

If there's one final test for a well-designed house, it's the presence of a good architect's signature on its plans. Unfortunately, only about one out of every four new houses today is designed by an architect, the biggest reason for no-design houses. Mention of architects also, to be sure, prompts skepticism in the minds of some people. They think of architects who are allegedly far more concerned with "aesthetics" than with designing a practical and economical house. This may well be true with some architects.

But by and large there are plenty of good architects around, and one is as essential for the planning of a really good house as a good engineer is essential for the planning of a bridge. If there's no architect, there's generally no design, in the true meaning of the word. Look for a good architect, and chances are you'll find a well-designed house, too.

The Garbled
Floor Plan

When you enter a house, ideally you should be able to go straight from one room to any other without passing through a third. If you must pass through a third room, it's a demerit. If you must cross the living room, it's one of the biggest sins. Think of the disruption it can cause when you're quietly entertaining guests and kids come barging through every time they enter or leave.

We know a couple whose biggest complaint about their house is its "Grand Central" living room. Located haphazardly in the center of the house, the living room must be used to get from the kitchen to the front door or to go upstairs. To get to the bathroom or to almost anywhere else in the house, they must also pass through the living room.

We know another couple whose biggest complaint is that their laundry room is located in the basement. They must make repeated trips down and back—to start the wash, answer the buzzer, transfer clothes to the dryer and so on. Never again will they have a house with a laundry away from the main post in the kitchen.

And we know of a woman who craves another house because her present house lacks a mud room. Particularly during bad weather, her children track in dust and dirt over freshly cleaned floors and rugs. A properly located mud room would permit the kids to get off their boots before walking through the rest of the house. Actually, it's not necessarily the lack of a mud room per se that causes the trouble. It's a bad floor plan that requires the children (and everybody else) entering the house to pass through various rooms before getting to an inside destination where they can shed dirty things and clean up.

These examples not only point up common troubles often encountered as a result of a garbled floor plan, but they also illustrate the importance of good circulation in a house, meaning the main traffic routes created by the basic floor plan. Good interior design also calls for proper zoning between each of the three main interior zones of a house—the living, sleeping and working quarters—and it calls for logical and sensible planning of each room.

Clearly, the way to avoid the garbled-plan trap is to know a little about what constitutes good interior design. Start with the basic floor plan, and see how well (or poorly) its circulation will work for your family. How can you tell when you look at a house?

■ SIX TESTS FOR GOOD CIRCULATION

The main traffic routes are the main paths the people in your family will use every day. They are the key to judging any house plan. Here they are:

1. *The main entrance*, the front door, should funnel people, mostly visitors, directly to the living room. An entrance foyer is highly recommended for receiving guests. A coat closet nearby is virtually essential. The main entrance should be quickly and easily accessible from the driveway and street in front. It should also be quickly accessible from the rooms inside, where you are likely to be when the doorbell rings, and especially from the kitchen. The kitchen-to-front-door route is one of the most frequently used

paths. A foyer is also important as a buffer or transfer chamber to keep howling winds, snow and rain from blowing into the heart of a house every time someone comes in the front door.

2. *A separate family entrance,* ordinarily a back or side door, should lead directly into the kitchen area. This is the door most used by a family itself, especially the children. A proper location is important to permit swift unloading of groceries, for example. It should also be located so that children can travel in and out easily and can quickly get to where they're going inside the house (such as a nearby bathroom). The route from the car to this entrance should be sheltered from rain and from snow and ice in a cold climate. But the route from this separate entrance to the kitchen should not run smack through the working area where the cooking takes place.

3. *The living room* should have a dead-end location for the reasons noted earlier plus a few others. It should not be a main route for everybody's travel around the house. Only then can you entertain guests in peace or just read or watch television without being continually disturbed by others walking through. Sometimes one end wall of the living room serves as a traffic lane; in effect, it's a hallway. That's all right if it happens to work in a particular house. Sometimes, though, a screen or half-wall may be necessary between it and the heart of the living room.

4. *The room arrangement* should be designed so that you can go from any room in the house to any other without going through a third room except possibly the dining room. Direct access to a bathroom from any room is particularly important. Yet in some houses this rule is violated to the consternation of its occupants, and there are even houses where access to a bedroom is possible only through a bathroom! If the bathroom is occupied, you are trapped in the bed-

room like a prisoner, unable to get out (unless you don't mind going out a window).

5.   *The kitchen* should be located centrally, not way out in a left-field corner of the house. In the kitchen one should be close to the front door, should be able to oversee children playing in the family room, say, or outside, and should be able to get to the dining room, the living room or the terrace without long hikes back and forth.

6.   *The main travel* routes between the house and the outdoor living areas—patio, terrace, deck or porch—should be short and direct. Can guests as well as family members go in and out easily? Is the outdoor area that you use most during pleasant weather easily accessible from the house? If it is, it will be used often. If not, you'll find it neglected and your family involuntarily depriving itself of outdoor-living benefits.

Those are the characteristics of a good floor plan. Because they're not always easy to get, there are many garbled plans. In fact, making a really efficient floor plan is one of the toughest things to do in the design of a house. This is why a good architect is essential. The importance of some of the individual tests will, of course, vary from family to family, depending on your own living habits and the activities you consider most important.

If you like to spend a lot of time outside the house, for example, you may place high importance on efficient access to the outdoors. If you entertain often, you will place importance on the design and location of the dining room and living room for entertaining. And so on. The way you live, therefore, should be taken seriously into account so that your house will simplify daily living activities and make life a lot more pleasant.

■ INTERIOR ZONING

Interior zoning is concerned with the logical arrangement of the rooms inside the house (see Figure 6.1). Ideally, every house should have three clear-cut zones to accommodate the three main kinds of activities: living, sleeping and working. The living zone embraces the living, dining and family rooms, where you engage in most activities other than working and sleeping. The work zone embraces the kitchen, laundry and perhaps a workshop, where obvious, if not unavoidable, work of one kind or another goes on. The sleeping zone embraces the bedrooms. Each zone should be separate from the other. The two-story house provides natural zoning between the bedrooms upstairs and the other rooms downstairs with natural benefits. On the other hand, a garbled split-level house can turn your life into a nightmare if, for example, the living or working zone is on more than one level with utter disregard for the way people live in a house.

Regardless of the kind of house, a buffer wall or other such separation is essential between the bedrooms and the other two zones, if for no other reason than to permit you to entertain guests without disturbing children at study or in bed at night. The kitchen and work zone should be separate from the living area. Can dishes be left stacked and unwashed there without being seen by guests in the living room? Can laundry be left unfinished but out of view when visitors call unexpectedly (or even when they are expected)? A "yes" answer to this question will tell you if a house plan has good zoning.

■ THE KITCHEN

The kitchen deserves top-priority attention. People usually spend more work time there than in any other single room. It also represents the highest-cost part of a house (because of its heavy-equipment concentration).

FIGURE 6.1 ■

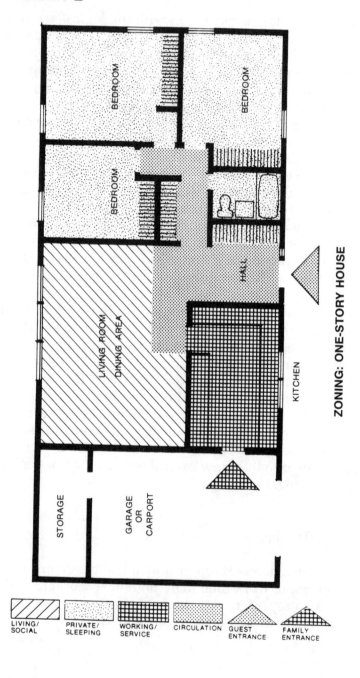

ZONING: ONE-STORY HOUSE

The kitchen more than any other room also tends to influence the resale value of your house. It is clearly important, and its design elements should be reported in some detail.

A central location is the first requisite, as noted earlier. The kitchen also rates a good exposure in relation to the sun. The same principles apply as those given in the preceding chapter for overall orientation of a house. Best kitchen exposure is one with windows on the southeast; next best is south. That will let most bright light and sunshine flood in during the day for at least the eight months of September to April. It will mean a bright, airy kitchen most of the time when you want it, yet the same exposure is easy to shade on hot summer days.

A kitchen facing east gets sun in the morning, but that's about all. One facing west gets little or no sun except in the afternoon, and in summer it will get hit with particularly hot afternoon sun. A northern exposure is darkest and gloomiest of all, receiving the least sun and light the year around. The same exposure principles also apply to a dining room or other area that is used for most meals.

Kitchen Work Triangle

The heart of a kitchen is its "work triangle," the arrangement of the refrigerator, sink and range in relation to each other. The entire process of efficiently preparing and cooking foods hinges on a good work triangle. From the refrigerator to sink to range should form a triangle with a total perimeter of at least 12 to 15 feet, but no more than 22 feet, according to research at Cornell University's renowned kitchen laboratory. The appliances should be at the points of the triangle to conform with the natural sequence of cooking.

Plenty of countertop space around the triangle is also a must. The Building Research Council at the University of Illinois recommends these minimum standards: at least 4½ feet of countertop length on the open-door side of the refrigerator between the refrigerator and the sink; 3½ to 4 feet of

FIGURE 6.2 ■

This compact kitchen displays the obligatory work triangle plan along with a creative design that uses limited space quite efficiently, very important in smaller houses. This award-winning design is by Cathy Larsen-Jepson, CKD, CBD; Bolig Kitchen Studio. (*Photo courtesy of the National Kitchen & Bath Association [NKBA] from the NKBA Design Competition.*)

countertop length between the sink and range; and at least 2 feet of countertop on the other side of the range. That adds up to a minimum of at least 10 feet of countertop length in all. An additional 2 feet of countertop is desirable, if not essential, at or near the range as a last-step serving center, where food is put on plates before being taken to the table. If either the refrigerator, the sink or the range is separate from the other triangle points—on a separate wall, for example—extra countertop space should be placed at its side, in addition to the minimum standards just given.

Make sure the refrigerator door opens the right way—toward the counter between the refrigerator and sink, so food can be conveniently unloaded where you will want it. The wrong-door refrigerator is a common flaw. A separate wall oven can go almost anywhere. Once it's loaded, it can usually be turned on without demanding attention until the bell rings. A location near the range is not essential, but because of its heat, it ordinarily should not be put flush next to the refrigerator.

An ample kitchen core and work triangle usually require a space at least 8 by 12 feet (96 square feet). That's the minimum to look for. With a dishwasher and separate oven, more space is needed. This should be an exclusive self-contained part of the kitchen out of the way of the main traffic routes used by people passing through the kitchen from one part of the house to another.

Kitchen Storage

According to studies at the University of Illinois, a minimum of at least 8½ running feet of wall cabinets and/or storage shelves is recommended for the kitchen. Another rule calls for at least 20 square feet of interior storage space under the countertop plus at least 10 square feet in wall cabinets. The proper cabinets and shelves should be located where they can house the particular items needed in each part of the kitchen—for example, storage for dishes and pots and pans near the sink and range; for working knives, bread box, flour, and other staples near the sink-refrigerator center, and so on.

Because kitchen cabinets can run into big money, consider open shelves for certain items. They can be a lot cheaper. If not enough cabinets or shelves are in a house, space should be available against walls or under the countertop to add what you'll need. The quality of cabinets is also important. You'll certainly want attractive cabinets with a rugged, hard finish that is easy to keep clean and will stay attractive over the years. The drawers should roll in and out

---

FIGURE 6.3 ■

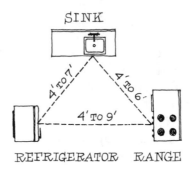

Kitchen work triangle shows minimum to maximum distances recommended for main work centers. (*All About Houses*)

easily, calling for nylon rollers; try them and see. The cabinet hardware and latches should be of good quality.

Final Checks for the Kitchen

Stand back and view the overall kitchen. It should be large enough to hold the table size required by your family, or an adequate dining area should be nearby. Some people also like space for a work desk and perhaps a sewing table. The laundry also should be nearby, or you may desire space in one part of the kitchen for a washer, dryer and ironing board.

Are there electric outlets spaced behind the countertop for convenient use of small appliances? If not, how will you operate a mixer, a blender and an electric frying pan as well as a toaster and a coffee maker? You'll want good lighting from above and lights that shed illumination over the full length of the countertop.

Finally, there's the need for good ventilation to keep the kitchen (as well as the rest of the house) free of cooking fumes and odors. A built-in exhaust fan is the least required. It should be located in the wall directly behind and above the range or in the ceiling directly over it. If located elsewhere, its exhaust efficiency will be low. A large range hood with built-in fan is even better. It should exhaust through a duct to outdoors. There are also "ventless" hoods equipped only with filters, with the hot air drawn through the filter and then spilled back into the kitchen; they do not cool a kitchen. Turn on the fan to check for noisy operation, a cause of widespread complaints. In a new house insist on a quiet one.

■ BATHROOM DESIGN

The location of the bathroom(s) is of first importance. There should be one located near the bedrooms. If it's the only one in the house, it should be convenient to other rooms as well.

Two or three bathrooms are usually essential for a large family, especially in a large or multilevel house. If an extra bathroom is wanted in a new house, order it when the house is being built, rather than after you move in. It can be installed for much less cost at that time than when the house is completed.

A big selling feature in new houses is the private bathroom for the master bedroom, but this is not always good design. In a two-bathroom house it might be better to locate the grown-ups' bathroom outside the master bedroom, where it is accessible to guests. Otherwise guests may be restricted to using the children's bathroom, which is often an embarrassing mess. Free the master bathroom, and the second bath can be given over completely to the children with no worry about the inevitable disorder found in it. This is unnecessary, of course, if a third bath or "powder room" is available for friends and visitors.

A full bathroom may be as small as 5 feet × 7 feet and a half-bath (powder room) as small as 24 inches × 40 inches or so. However, the key to adequate bathroom size is not the dimensions necessarily but the number of people who are likely to be using it, particularly during the hectic morning rush hour. The more baths, the smaller the load on each and the less the need for large baths. You can usually tell by sight if a bathroom is large enough to handle two or three children or two grown-ups at once.

But extra bathrooms are not always necessary. A double lavatory, for example, may save you the expense of an extra bathroom. Two lavatories side by side can provide double-duty service from one bathroom. Sometimes equipping a bathroom with two toilet compartments can be adequate and less costly than an extra bath. These are especially good ideas for large families.

The quality of the fixtures in the bathroom is also important, and this is taken up in Chapter 8.

■ OTHER ROOMS

A room should look and "feel" bright, cheerful and pleasant. The presence of properly designed windows can make a huge difference. There should be enough unbroken wall area for easy furniture placement. Rooms should be large enough to accept your furniture. Good heating, adequate wiring and lighting are also points to check. As for size and location, here are some minimum standards from the Building Research Council at the University of Illinois.

- A living room at least 12 feet × 20 feet, with at least 10 feet to 12 feet of unbroken wall for a couch. Remember, the living room should not be a major highway for traffic through the house, and the front door of the house should not open directly into it.

- A family room of at least 12 feet × 16 feet, though 12 feet × 20 feet is better. It should be on the same level as the kitchen and near, if not adjacent to, the kitchen.

- Bedrooms at least 9 feet × 11½ feet, with at least 4 square feet of closet space per person. The bedrooms should have privacy from the rest of the house, and the master bedroom in particular should have built-in privacy from the children's bedrooms. You'll notice, in fact, that almost every notable custom house published in architectural magazines will have the master bedroom located apart from other bedrooms, if not by itself on the other side of the house from children's rooms. Though it's not always easy to do in a low-priced house, it can be an excellent design feature in nearly every house.

Twenty-Two Common Little House Design Traps

The little things also count in a house. Here is a list of common design flaws found in houses; it includes a few already noted in this chapter, repeated here because of their importance:

1. No separate entranceway or foyer to receive visitors.

2. No opening in the front door, or no window or glass outlook alongside that lets you see who's at the door.

3. No roof overhang or similar protection over the front door for shelter from rainy weather.

4. No direct access route from the driveway to the kitchen.

5. No direct route from outdoors to a bathroom so children can come in and out with minimum of bother and mud-tracking.

6. Gas, electric, and water meters inside the house or in the garage or basement, rather than outside. Outside meters do away with the need to let meter readers in every month.

7. Fishbowl picture window in the front of the house, exposing you to every passerby.

8. The nightmare driveway that opens out on a blind curve so you cannot see oncoming traffic when back-

ing out. A driveway that slopes up to the street is almost as bad, especially for trapping you hopelessly on a winter morning when your car won't start.

9. Isolated garage or carport with no direct or protected access from car to house.

10. Accident-inviting doors that open toward the basement stairs.

11. Cut-up rooms with windows haphazardly located. Sometimes too many doors make it impossible to arrange furniture.

12. Windows in children's rooms that are too low for safety, too high to see out of, and/or too small or difficult to get out of in case of fire.

13. A hard-to-open window, usually the double-hung type, over the kitchen sink. An easily cranked casement window is usually best here; a sliding window second best.

14. A window over the bathroom tub. This generally causes cold drafts as well as rotted windowsills as a result of condensation.

15. Stage-front bathrooms placed squarely in view of a space like the living room or smack in view at the top of the stairway. Ideally, one should be able to go from any bedroom to the bathroom without being seen from another part of the house.

16. Only one bathroom, especially tough on you in a two-story or split-level house.

17. No light switches at every room entrance and exit.

18. No light or electrical outlet on a porch, deck, patio or terrace.

19. No outside light to light up the front path to and from the house.

20. Noisy light switches that go on and off like a pistol shot. Silently operating switches cost only a little more, and no new house can be called modern without them today.

21. Child-trap closets that can't be opened from inside.

22. Small economy-size closets that are hardly big enough for half your wardrobe. Also watch out for narrow closet doors that keep half of the closet out of reach without a fishing pole; basket-ball-player shelves too high for a person of normal height; and clothes poles so low that dresses and trousers cannot hang without hitting the floor.

It should be clear by now that good design involves more than merely good looks (often deceptive) and surface glamour. The difference between a good design and the garbled-plan trap has to do with how well the house will work for you and your family.

The famous architect Le Corbusier aptly said that a house should be a "machine for living." His words stirred immediate anger in some circles where people reacted violently to the impersonal inference. Nonetheless it's an excellent phrase to remember when you inspect a house. Will the house serve you efficiently and well? Is it designed to permit you to carry out your everyday activities with ease and convenience in addition to providing pleasant and cheerful surroundings? Or is it a garbled plan that makes everyday activities a continual chore and burden?

If the plan is truly efficient, logically and sensibly designed for humans, it will come far closer to being a genuinely personal house. It will provide much satisfaction and continual pleasure every day you are in it. It will not be a garbled-plan trap.

■ ═══ CHAPTER 7 ═══ ■

The Old-House Lemon

The experience of a young couple illustrates a common (and sad) mishap with old houses. By old houses, we mean any used house one year or older. The couple bought a large, old three-story house in downstate Illinois. It was on a pleasant street and was priced at a mere $84,500. It was rather rundown, they knew, but they were both young and eager to go to work on the house. It was a challenge. Besides, where else could they find such a big house at such a low price?

Taking stock of things two years later, they found they had poured more than $45,000 into the house, excluding their own labor over many nights and weekends. Yet there were still improvements to be made. It was a particularly cold winter, and it was then that the old furnace chose to fail, requiring another $2,500 for a replacement.

That was too much. They decided to throw in the towel and sell it for enough to get their money back and find another house. Then came the final blow. The most they could get for the house was $110,000, which meant a loss that they could ill afford. They had been trapped by an old-house lemon.

They had made two mistakes. They had underestimated the amount of repairs and improvements that were needed, and they had overimproved the house for its location. As a result, they found that the value of the house did not grow, dollar for dollar, with the money they had poured into it.

■ WHAT IS AN "OLD" HOUSE?

There are three kinds of old houses. The first, the kind we would all like, is the old house—again any age—that is in good or excellent condition. The second is the kind that looks deceptively sturdy and solid but contains serious flaws that are often difficult to detect. This group includes houses that were built recently. It's hard to believe that anything could go wrong with them in such a short time, but their budding troubles usually started as a result of bad initial construction, or the house was put up by a vanishing builder, and the defects, like a progressive disease, take a little time to develop serious symptoms. Sometimes the first owners discover their mistake and decide to get out from under and unload the place on another unsuspecting buyer.

The third kind of old house is the relic. Its run-down condition is far more obvious, however proud a house it was in the past. The perplexing thing is that people continually buy such houses with the delusion that they've discovered a rare bargain. Such a buyer knows that the house requires inevitable repairs and improvements. "But once fixed up," he says to his wife (or vice versa), "it will be a splendid house. Besides, it's loaded with charm." A psychological compulsion apparently drives certain people into buying the old relic.

The moment of truth occurs when all those repairs and all that modernization not only are found to be inevitable but also add up to a whopping expense far beyond any initial estimates. Sometimes the old relic is so far gone that it is hopelessly irretrievable. The only realistic solution is to tear it down and build anew.

■ WHY BUY AN OLD HOUSE?

There are nevertheless good reasons for buying some old houses. Many offer much more space than a new house at the same price, and all those rooms can hold irresistible appeal. An old house is often the only house available within convenient commuting distance of a job downtown in the city. The new houses being built are too far out in distant suburbs. Often an old house can be occupied immediately with little or no work required. There may be practically no moving-in expenses or costs for a new lawn, landscaping or anything else of the kind associated with new houses. And with an old house you can generally move into an established neighborhood, with shade trees on the streets and little likelihood of new taxes like those often levied on new houses in expanding new suburbs.

It is also often remarked that old houses were built much better than new houses are, but this is frequently a myth. People will offer those old clichés, saying, "They don't build houses the way they used to," or, "You can't beat an old house for solid construction." To be sure, many splendid old houses boast thick old stone walls, handsome oak-plank flooring and other nostalgic features like high ceilings, tile roofs and hand-carved woodwork. They are lovely features of a bygone age, seldom duplicated in new houses today (see Figures 7.1 and 7.2).

The other side of the coin, however, is that new houses come with many features unknown in old houses: exciting modern kitchens and bathrooms, central heating and air-conditioning, fuel-saving insulation, and rugged new materials and products that were formerly unknown but can now make a house exceedingly pleasant to live in. As far as the basic structure goes, a good new house today can be as strong, sturdy and durable as the best old house, if not more so.

An old house, however good, can also be difficult to buy because of the difficulty of financing it. You won't get the benefits of the financing incentives that builders offer new homebuyers. But by far the biggest pitfall to avoid is the

FIGURE 7.1 ■

Before. The old house, built in Piermont, New York, in 1840, went begging for a buyer. Like other relics, it represented a good buy only at the right price and only to people with the talent, willingness and money to restore it to its original splendor. Priced for sale at $16,000 in the late 1950s, and probably not worth it, the owner finally sold it for $8,200. (*Photo: Don Blauhut*)

old-house lemon, the kind that is riddled with shortcomings (to put it mildly) and in many cases is suffering from senility.

Obsolescence rates special mention. The older the house, the more likely vital parts will be worn and run down. The usual furnace will last 15 to 20 years, more or less, and repairs if not total replacement are inevitable. The usual roof covering is good for about the same period of time, after which it begins to crack and dry out, leaks start up, and a new roof cover must be bought. The wiring circuits become worn and frayed over the years and grow increasingly inadequate to handle all the new appliances and other electrical equipment that we pile into our homes. These and a variety of other items inevitably fall prey to wear and tear over the years, with the house naturally becoming less functional (though some owners refuse to admit it).

FIGURE 7.2 ■

After. The same house restored and modernized—now the Blauhut house in Piermont—is a handsome and spacious example of nineteenth-century Federal architecture. *(Photo: Don Blauhut)*

Every house requires upkeep, maintenance and periodic modernization, but not every one gets it. On this score there's a special kind of old house to watch for warily. It's the one that has been in a family for years, though the children have long since grown up and left. The one or two surviving older people who stayed with the house do not mind a kitchen that is increasingly outmoded. There's only one operating bathroom, but that, too, is perfectly adequate for the small demands put on it. That kind of house for sale should flash a red danger flag before your eyes.

If you move in with a large family, it will soon become apparent that the house is incapable of meeting the heavy new demands put on it. Though formerly adequate for one or two older people, the plumbing will groan and begin to slow down because of the new strain put on it by a large active family. The furnace or the water heater or both, also asked to meet heavier demands for heating and hot water, will be forced to put out more, but neither can heat very well anymore. Similarly, the wiring and other parts of the house that formerly could keep going under mild operating conditions are not capable of coping with new technology, including computers, televisions, and stereos occupants introduce to the house. A variety of ailments sprout.

■ HOW TO AVOID THE OLD-HOUSE LEMON

How can you distinguish between the used house that's in fundamentally good condition and one that is not? There is only one surefire test. Have the house inspected by an expert. A satisfactory house inspection is a common contingency in purchase contracts. The cost will ordinarily run from about $200 to $400 or more, depending on house price and other variables. The inspector should prepare a detailed written report on the condition of the structure and mechanical systems. You should also ask for estimates on the cost of correcting problems.

Such engineers are found in the telephone classified pages under "Home Inspection Services" or "Building Inspection Firms." Some inspection consultants are quite good; others are not so good, so ask around for recommendations and check inspectors' qualifications before hiring one.

Your real estate agent can tell you about inspectors in your area but may not be the best source for a recommendation. You should have no doubt that the inspector's loyalty lies with you, not the agent or the homeseller.

One way to screen inspectors is to check their professional affiliations. The two major associations for home inspectors are the American Society of Home Inspectors and the National Institute of Building Inspectors. Inspectors must meet professional education standards before gaining membership to the organizations. You can ask inspectors about the specific requirements for these accreditations. Request references from previous clients as well.

Using an expert is also recommended even when you buy a new house. The expert can judge the quality of construction for you and also spot inadvertent mistakes and construction oversights that you would overlook. With the expert's report in hand you can request the builder to make the necessary corrections. The builder will usually be happy to do so before you buy the house (in order to make the sale) but perhaps not so willing after you buy.

■ HOW MUCH WILL THE HOUSE REALLY COST?

The next step is to determine the cost of essential repairs and modernization. If it is truly a fine old house, this cost should be small, but most houses require some work of one kind or another. Any way you look at it, a $125,000 house that requires $30,000 worth of work is a $155,000 house. It's as simple as that.

An old house in run-down condition can still be a bargain if its price plus the cost of essential work adds up to a reasonable figure. Of course, your total estimated investment in the house should be reflected in increased value. You don't want to overimprove unless you intend to remain in the place for many years.

■ ENVIRONMENTAL HAZARDS IN THE HOME

Environmental hazards in the home are not confined to used houses. However, certain building materials that we now consider to be potentially dangerous were at one time widely used in residential construction. Therefore you should be on the watch for potential environmental hazards when inspecting used houses. If you're looking for a fixer-upper to rehab, you should be particularly attentive to potential risks because whether completely gutting the building or simply scraping paint, you may be releasing dangerous dust particles into the air that you and your family breathe.

Most states now have disclosure laws requiring the seller to reveal any known environmental problems with the home. Even if your state does not have such a law, if you ask the seller about environmental problems in or around the house, he or she has a legal obligation to answer your question honestly. Because lenders share in the risk of a property, some are beginning to require environmental tests such as radon screening as part of the property evaluation process. Of course, the expression "buyer beware" always applies to real estate. A seller may not know about an environmental problem or may choose not to disclose it despite the law. When selecting a home inspector, you should ask if they will help you identify common environmental hazards and if they have any special training or certification to do so. The federal government and other agencies publish plenty of free or low-cost information about environmental hazards. Your regional Environmental Protection Agency (EPA) or state health department is a good place to start. If you're having trouble locating these sources, contact your local library. Below is information about three of the most common risks—radon, lead and asbestos.

Radon

No home, new or used, in any part of the country is free from the risk of radon. Radon-222 is an odorless, invisible radioactive gas released from the ground. According to the EPA, 1 out of 15 homes have high radon levels. The average radon level in U.S. homes is 1.5 pCi/l. You should take action to reduce radon if the level is higher than 4 pCi/l.

High radon levels increase your risk of lung cancer, especially if you or others in your household smoke.

Ask the seller if the house has been tested for radon. If so, find out where and when the test was taken, what the results were and if any action was taken to correct high levels. You can use the results of the seller's test or request that another test be taken. Be sure to use a certified radon tester. You may want to specify that it be a tamper-proof test, which costs around $300.

Radon levels are highest in the basement. Therefore, that is where short-term testing should be done. If the house doesn't have a basement, use the lowest living area of the house. You can buy short-term testing kits in a hardware store. Make sure any kit you purchase indicates that it meets EPA requirements, and follow the instructions on the packaging. However, if you suspect a problem and are seriously interested in purchasing the house, it makes sense to use a professional, who in addition to identifying a problem can advise you on the cost of correcting it.

Radon can enter the home through cracks in concrete slabs, floors, walls or caulking, around loose fitting pipes, floor or wall cracks. It is also in some well water. Simple measures to increase ventilation can reduce radon levels significantly. You should also seal cracks in the basement floor or around pipes. Radon is controllable. Costs vary significantly depending on the nature and extent of the problem and can run anywhere from several hundred dollars to about $3,000 or more. In contrast, taking special radon control measures in new home construction runs just about $350 to $500.

Lead

Though the biggest lead problems are in low-income public housing, middle-class homeowners are in no way exempt. Before World War II, lead was common in house paints. About one-third of the houses built between 1940 and 1960 contain lead paint. It was not until 1978 that lead beyond minuscule amounts was banned in the manufacture of paint for residential use. So if a house was built prior to 1980, there is a good possibility it contains lead paint.

Lead is harmful to many human body systems. Children, with their developing nervous systems and brains, are particularly vulnerable. With habits like crawling on floors and carpeting, playing near window sills, and putting things in their mouths, children are also more likely to come in contact with lead. Because their bodies are smaller, they are sensitive to smaller amounts. Pregnant women should be just as cautious as parents of small children, because lead is carried through the blood and can harm an unborn child.

Many people buy older homes, planning major remodeling or renovation projects. But renovating a home with lead-based paint can be dangerous without proper, sometimes expensive, precautions. Scraping, sanding or heating lead-based paint will release harmful amounts of lead into the air. A fine dust will settle on floors or carpeting and will go right back into the air with vacuuming or sweeping.

Lead paint tends to crack in a regular, square-like pattern. Other factors, however, might cause these same symptoms. The Residential Lead-based Paint Hazard Reduction Act (also called Title X), which went into effect in 1995, requires that sellers disclose the known presence of lead-based paint to their prospective buyers. If you buy a home built before 1978, the law requires that you be given 10 days in which to obtain a lead hazard risk assessment or inspection, and your sales contract should contain a lead warning statement. You should be able to get a lead paint inspection for a couple hundred dollars.

Lead can be a difficult problem to correct. Painting over a lead-based paint is not sufficient. Removal should be done by qualified professionals. Another solution is to encapsulate the affected surfaces with a solid fireproof barrier, such as drywall. For windows and doors, replacement can be a cost-effective solution. Windows with lead-based paint can be particularly hazardous because the opening and closing loosens chips and dust particles.

Another potential source of lead is the water, where it might be picked up from the municipal water supply and service pipes or from piping in the house itself. You can call your local health department for information about water testing, offered sometimes as a free service.

Asbestos

Asbestos is a fibrous mineral that has been a frequently used material in houses because it is strong, durable, fire retardant and an excellent insulator. Studies have shown that workers exposed to a large amount of asbestos showed an increased risk of cancer. It is less certain how dangerous the levels found in most homes can be. However, experts have been unable to prove that it is completely safe.

Since 1979, the use of asbestos in home construction materials has been reduced substantially. Prior to 1973, asbestos was commonly used in such items as floor coverings, ceiling tile, duct wrapping on heating and air-conditioning systems, insulation on hot water pipes and boilers, and fireproofing. If you're looking at an older home, chances are it does contain asbestos. Its use may be obvious in certain areas such as insulation of visible pipes. The only way to be completely sure is to hire a qualified professional to survey the home and test the material. You may also be able to collect a sample yourself and send it to a lab for testing. Health departments or EPA offices can supply a list of labs and testers.

Asbestos is only dangerous when it is friable (when deterioration causes it to loosen, crumble and flake). It's minuscule fibers will then be released in the air and will lodge in the lungs when inhaled. If the asbestos is in good shape, there is little risk, and the best thing to do is leave it alone. You can make minor repairs on pipe or duct insulation yourself, using paint, duct tape or sealant, though proceed with caution. Always avoid scraping, sanding, sawing, cutting or drilling any material that contains asbestos. You should also be careful about asbestos in areas that could be disturbed, such as where children play. If you're planning a major remodelling project, you will need to hire qualified contractors to remove the asbestos-containing material. The EPA and some states train and certify contractors. You should call your local health department or state agencies for information. It is estimated that asbestos removal will cost three times as much as if the material did not contain asbestos. The cost can run from $1,500 up to several thousand dollars.

■ THE MOST COMMON OLD-HOUSE AILMENTS

Following is a listing of the most common defects found in used homes. Some of the common defects listed are found in young houses, too, including some of the most recently built used houses for sale.

The list adds up to nearly a dozen widespread flaws encountered in existing houses, but don't be alarmed by the number. You may encounter no more than two or three in a typical used house (excluding the old relic). This list can alert you to some of the costs of fixing up a house, and your inspector can also give you potential costs. To get an accurate estimate for a fixing up a house, however, you must call in a contractor.

1 and 2. Old-fashioned kitchens and run-down bathrooms. These are the two most prevalent shortcomings in old houses. You can judge the condition of each simply by looking. How much modernization will be required will depend on your personal standards. The kitchen in a house may satisfy you or may not. Don't kid yourself, though. Make a realistic appraisal of these key rooms.

Full renovation of an obsolete old kitchen will ordinarily cost about $15,000 to $25,000 and more if you want the very latest and best kitchen and everything else that signifies. A new full bath, installed where there was none before, can cost about $6,000 to $12,000. The cost of remodeling a full old bathroom can range from $5,000 to $15,000, and more with luxury features.

3. Run-down heating.   If the house is hard to heat, fuel bills run astronomically high. Even then you still suffer chilly discomfort. Insulation and the kind of heat also enter the picture here. Because this problem is so common and ranks as a major trap, it is dealt with in detail in Chapter 9.

4. Defective septic-tank system.   If the house plumbing does not empty into a city sewer line, it usually empties into a septic-tank system or a cesspool. Determining the operating condition of the system is not always easy. If a house has a septic tank, ask the owners how well it works. Sometimes they'll say it's fine, though it isn't. Other times they'll frankly say that it isn't as good as it should be, but you can live with it until new city sewers are installed. Hooking up to a sewer will cost at least a few hundred dollars. You can also call the local public health office and ask them how well septic tanks work in the area. Have serious troubles been experienced? Ordinarily they will know because of the health hazard involved.

The condition of a house cesspool may also be hard to determine. Some of them work for years without trouble; others don't. Like septic tanks, how well a cesspool works depends largely on the kind of soil. A porous soil that drains well is a good sign because it readily absorbs sewage overflow. A hard, claylike soil is a bad sign. You can get further indication of possible trouble by determining—again from a good source like the health-department people—the kind of soil-drainage characteristics in the area and whether or not cesspools work well there.

5. Wet basement.   The basic problem stems from a chronic wet-soil condition coupled with poor drainage around a house. So much water piles up in the ground around a house that there is nowhere for it to go except to press through the foundation walls into the basement. Ordinary black asphalt waterproofing plastered on the walls won't necessarily keep it out either.

The problem is encountered most with a house located in low-lying ground, in a valley, or in an area surrounded by higher ground or hills from which rainwater flows down through underground streams. Conversely, a house set on a bluff or high ground is more likely to stay dry. So look around at the terrain for the telltale high-ground sources of shed water that can endanger the basement. Ask the owner if the basement stays dry after a heavy rain (again, you may or may not get an honest answer). But the answers can be revealing. Check the basement yourself for signs of water stains, particularly on the walls facing the high ground outside. A chronic wet basement should be avoided, because it can cause wood-rot problems and spread mildew throughout the house.

Sometimes, however, the problem is easily licked simply by improving the soil drainage around the house, a procedure that costs very little. Sometimes you can do it yourself with a shovel. Often it's caused by defective downspout runoff of water from the roof, and this, too, is relatively easy and inexpensive to correct. If the problem is chronic, however, the remedy can cost a couple thousand dollars or more. The ground must be dug up all around the foundation walls, the walls must be properly waterproofed and, in addition, a new drain-tile system must be installed in the ground outside the foundation footing (the base of the house).

6. Puny wiring.   The older the house, the more likely the wiring is obsolete and inadequate. This is because of the skyrocketing electrical demands in houses as a result of the hordes of new appliances that have been introduced. In 1940, for example, only a dozen or so different kinds of electrical items were used in the home. A mere 30-ampere electric service was all you needed to power a house, including the lights. Now there are close to a hundred different electric devices of one kind or another found in the home— everything from washers and dryers to televisions, computers and microwave ovens. Some of them, such as an electric dryer or a range, draw more electricity than could be supplied by the entire electric board in a 1940 house.

The average house today requires an electric service input of 240 volts and 100 amperes capacity. It should say at least that—240 volts, 100 amperes—on the main electric switchbox. That's where the fuses or circuit breakers are located. If it's a large house or if it has heavy electric users like electric heat or air-conditioning or, say, an electric range or a dryer, you should look for at least 240 volts and 150 to 200 amperes capacity.

Inspect the main electric board. If it's a small one with a rating of less than 100 amperes, a new electric service is likely to be needed. The cost will run from about $500 to $750. You are also likely to need rewiring, if not new wiring circuits, new switches and new outlets in various parts of the house. Figure around $50 apiece for each new switch and double outlet you'll need, plus $75 to $100 roughly for each new heavy-appliance outlet needed for equipment like an electric dryer. In all, the total cost of new wiring for a typical seven- or eight-room house could run a couple thousand dollars, and more for a larger house.

7. Clogged-up plumbing.   Clogged-up plumbing is most likely found in houses built prior to World War II, because corrosion-resistant copper and bronze plumbing was not introduced for housing until just before World War II. Before then, iron and steel pipes were the rule. Over several decades such piping tends to choke up with rust and corrosion, like cholesterol chokes off the blood flow in human arteries. In time, little or no water can get through, and the plumbing must be replaced. Some younger houses in certain areas will also have iron or steel plumbing pipes, which is not a good sign. Nonferrous copper or bronze pipes last much longer.

A small magnet can let you know the kind of piping in a house, assuming it is not evident to the eye. Hold the magnet near the pipes. It will be drawn to iron or steel but not to copper or bronze.

If the plumbing consists of an old set of iron or steel pipes, chances are it is going downhill, particularly if the water only trickles out of the faucets. Turn all the faucets on at once in a bathroom (an upstairs bathroom in a multifloor house). Make it a real test by flushing the toilet at the same time. If the water slows to a trickle, it's not good. It could well signify serious trouble. New plumbing can cost a few thousand dollars, and more for a large house.

Sometimes, however, low water pressure is caused by insufficient water pressure from the street. Actually, this problem is usually caused by too small a water-supply line to' the house from the street. A new and larger line is the remedy at a cost ranging from about $500 to perhaps thrice that, depending on the digging distance from the house to the street water line.

8. Termite and wood-rot damage.   First, there's no need to panic if there are termites. They may have entered relatively recently, and it usually takes a few years before they get a foothold in a house and cause real damage. If, however, they've been having a ball inside the house for some time, things can be quite serious. You may not discover the party going on until the piano falls through a weakened floor.

Termites have now spread to virtually every state in the nation except Alaska. They can burrow into the substructure of a house through cracks and holes a mere 1/32 inch in diameter. They usually come up from the ground below the house, and that means coming up into cement-floor houses (no basements) with virtually no visible signs of their arrival. You can't see them unless you happen on one of their camouflaged little mud tunnels and break it open, or cut into a beam they've infiltrated. An expert, however, knows where to look for them. A minor termite condition can sometimes be corrected for a few hundred dollars, but a major one can require several thousand dollars worth of repairs.

Wood rot is often mistaken for termite damage because of the similarity of appearance. It is caused by a fungus that attacks wood, eating and dismembering it much like termites. It causes even more widespread damage than termites and can call for much timber replacement in a house.

The inspector you hire for a termite check should also give you a report on the extent, if any, of wood rot.

9. *Sagging structure.* Every house will settle a little over the years. But if the structure is wrenched severely out of shape, something drastic is wrong. Stand back a few feet from each corner of the house and sight down each of the four walls. The lines should be square and true. A major bulge or awkward protuberance can spell trouble. A few inches out of plumb can be expected and is usually of no importance. Notice if the windows and doors line up squarely with each other and with the house frame. Windows and doors should open and close easily—that is, they should not bind.

What you see can indicate whether or not a house is in serious trouble. A contractor can estimate the cost of repairs. Some new supporting posts in the cellar may be all that's needed at relatively low cost. Major work on the underpinnings can cost several thousand dollars.

10. *Worn-out roof and rain gutters.* The condition of the roof can usually be judged simply by looking for broken, cracked or missing shingles. Take a close look at the flashing around the chimney. That's where the first leaks generally show up. A typical asphalt-shingle roof, the most common cover on houses, will ordinarily last 15 to 20 years before reroofing is required. It may wear out faster in the hot South, where the overhead sun is extremely intense, and last longer in northern states. A roof more than 15 to 20 years old is likely to be a trouble spot.

The cost of new roofing for an old house can vary widely based on the roofing material used, local labor costs and the kind of roof being covered. The total cost of a new roof for an average house will run about $2,500 to $5,000. Gutters can be troublesome, too, especially if they are leaky, broken or just worn out. Figure another $600 to $1,200 for new gutters.

11. Worn-out water heater.   Replacing this essential little item is a comparatively small expense: $300 to $600. But it's a common one. Many water heaters are undersized, so you run out of hot water in the middle of a shower, bath or clothes wash. A good many low-grade water heaters are found in houses. They sometimes last no more than three to four years, then spring a leak and must be replaced.

Check the water heater for adequate capacity. Most families require a 40-to-50-gallon tank, though 30 gallons may be large enough if the nameplate says it is a "rapid recovery" model. Those are minimum capacities for gas and oil models. Electric water heaters should range from 80 gallons capacity and up. A smaller 60-gallon size will do only if the nameplate says it's a "high speed" or "high watt" model or if your family is small and has modest hot-water needs.

Also check the condition of the heater. The first signs of impending failure are rust and cracks at the bottom of the tank and sometimes a small leak, with water running onto the floor. You can check these things by looking at the bottom of the unit with a flashlight.

■ THE FINAL JUDGMENT

A few final words about buying an old house. It's a good idea to spend an hour or two going over the house, even though you plan to hire an expert for a professional inspection. This is not to say that you should be your own expert. But a professional inspection will cost a few hundred dollars. A personal inspection can give you a good insight into the house and help you narrow the field to a house or two for professional inspection.

Besides the common flaws just listed, notice the condition of the house inside and out. Are the floors and woodwork in good shape? How do the attic and basement shape up? What about the workmanship? Look at the floor around the bathroom tub and shower and at the kitchen floor below the sink and at the base of the cabinets. These are chronic splash-water areas, where evidence of rot and deterioration often shows up first. Observe the condition of the foundation walls. Does the masonry contain many cracks and holes? (A few are inevitable in nearly every house.) In short, give the place a good, if not expert, going-over.

How do you feel now about the condition of the house? Right here you will begin to get a distinct impression of the house. If you have nagging doubts about it, don't push them out of your mind simply because you want to like the house. When you get home, sit down and let your true feelings rise to the surface. A husband and wife can exchange views. Is it really a good house, or does it spell trouble? It may have a few flaws, but practically every house does. Is it really worth the price asked? Or is it worth buying only if you get it at a reduced price (to allow for repairs)?

Ask yourself questions like these as you reflect about the house, and then answer them realistically. Sure, some houses are not all you may like them to be, but if your standards are set too high, you may never find one that will suit. On the other hand, what your deep-down feelings honestly are about the house, whether it is really a good one for you or not, can be the best indication of whether or not to buy it.

The key to this judgment is facing up to your basic feelings about the house and recognizing them for what they are. If you realize that the house stirs serious doubts in you, watch out; but if the house has been checked by an expert, if it has no serious flaws, and if you really like it and want it, then you've found a good house.

■ WARRANTY POLICIES FOR USED HOUSES

A serious potential defect sometimes can, of course, go undiscovered even by a Sherlock Holmes checking a used house for you. One source of protection is a warranty policy that covers major unexpected repair costs for a year, but these policies are not total insurance. Some cover only the major structural, mechanical and electrical parts of the house, and things like termite damage are not covered.

Oftentimes sellers or their listing brokers will offer a one-year warranty policy. The insurance serves their interest because it is a sales incentive and lessens the likelihood of lawsuits from unhappy buyers. If you're interested in such a policy, you may be able to get your seller to pay for it.

■ ══ CHAPTER 8 ══ ■

The Marginal House

The marginal house is the one that just squeaks by. The quality of its construction and the parts that went into it are marginal. It's not necessarily a substandard house. The house very likely comes up to the local building code and sometimes even FHA's minimum standards, but nevertheless it's a marginal house.

This is no news to the knowledgeable homeowner who has bought one or more houses, particularly if one was a low-quality cracker box. It could also have been a supposedly good house of higher-than-average cost. One such couple knows well the trouble, irritation and extra expense a marginal house represents. There was the summer vacation that went down the drain because money was needed for a new paint job, though at the time the house was a mere three years old. There were the children's chilly bedrooms that were impossible to heat during cold weather, in spite of the high fuel bills. There were the paper-thin walls and the cheap paneling that looked deceptively handsome when they first moved in but soon began to wear thin and look tawdry like cheap wallpaper. And there was also the low-grade flooring, especially in the kitchen and bathroom, that was impossible to keep clean and good-looking.

■ WHY SO MUCH MARGINAL QUALITY?

There is so much marginal quality because nearly every-thing that goes into a house—the flooring, wall products, roofing, siding, heating, wiring, paint and virtually every other product—can be had in more than one grade or in some cases more than one weight or thickness. Naturally, the lowest grade costs the least in initial price, just as the lowest-grade beef and eggs and the cheapest quality of clothing material carry the lowest price tags. The lowest-grade economy materials are used widely in house con-struction to keep down costs. They are designed to meet cer-tain minimum standards. What's more, marginal quality is not limited to low-priced houses. It's also prevalent to a degree in many high-priced houses, including luxury houses.

The lowest-grade marginal products actually cost you money in the long run and often in the short run, too. In time their performance trails off. They require more and more upkeep and maintenance and time and expense. They usually have a shorter life than the high-quality grades of the same products. That can call for early replacements, again with the homeowner paying extra. All these things add up to a marginal house that becomes a growing source of nagging annoyance and bother. Moreover, really good if not top-notch quality building products often cost only a lit-tle more than the lowest-grade ones. You don't have to pay Cadillac prices for top construction quality. The very best quality house paint, for example, costs only a few dollars more per gallon than the minimal grade usually used on houses. Using that best paint on an average-size house will increase the total paint cost by only $100 or so. The cost of the labor to apply the paint does not increase. Yet you get a far more durable exterior paint job that will last up to twice as long as marginal paint, and that means, among other things, reduced repainting expenses.

High-quality flooring, paneling, wiring, heating and other products cost only a little more, by and large, than the same products in marginal quality. Like top-notch paint,

FIGURE 8.1 ■

High-quality flooring is essential for attractive long-lasting floors. This quarry tile is an excellent material for the heavily trafficked entrance of a house. A few handsome, high-quality features and products like this, obvious at first glance, generally indicate a high-quality house, as opposed to a questionable or marginal house. (*All About Houses*)

each is more durable, lasts longer and requires less upkeep, cleaning and maintenance than its marginal-quality counterpart, and the cost of installing high-quality materials is generally no greater than the cost of installing marginal materials. Virtually the same amount of labor is required to put down a new floor, for example, regardless of whether the best- or worst-quality flooring is used. The principle of quality also applies to such things as the masonry work, like the foundation of a house. High-quality masonry simply requires the use of a few extra bags of cement in the mix, raising the construction cost of a typical house by about $50 to $60, and that's all.

■ THE COST OF QUALITY

Studies show that the construction cost of a new house built with high-quality products and materials will run no more than 10 percent to 12 percent more than the cost of the same house built with marginal parts. That excludes extra money spent for top-of-the-line luxury items, like gold-plated bathroom fittings with super-high price tags for their fashionable looks. None of their extra cost goes for additional performance quality. And it excludes spending extra for such things as premium oak floors that can indeed contribute to a handsome interior. But it doesn't necessarily add to construction quality.

Spending money chiefly for increased construction quality—as detailed later in this chapter—can pay for itself in reduced upkeep, maintenance and repair bills, in reduced housekeeping, as well as in longer, trouble-free life and performance from virtually everything in the house, including literally the kitchen sink.

An obvious example is the sharply reduced energy bills that result by spending extra for high energy efficiency in a house, as noted later in Chapter 9. The extra money spent for energy efficiency pays for itself in energy savings within a comparatively few years. The savings every year afterward is money in the bank. And it's after-tax money, too!

A growing number of mortgage lenders also give homebuyers a special break or two on the mortgage terms for houses with high energy efficiency. They are by no means being altruistic. It's a hard-nosed, realistic business policy. Because of reduced monthly energy bills, these homebuyers will have an easier time paying off their mortgages. In short, they are better mortgage risks! This is something to ask about when you shop for a mortgage on an energy-efficient house that you may build or buy. A house built with high-quality construction should also benefit from increased resale value, a fact that also could be cited when mortgage shopping.

In sum, the high-quality house makes sense in every way. Conversely, the marginal house is a snare and a trap—a snare because it costs less at first and a trap because it ends up costing you more, sometimes considerably more (when major things wear out and must be replaced at high expense). Money aside, the high-quality house really pays for itself in the extra satisfaction and living benefits that you receive, as with virtually any other high-quality product you may buy.

■ HOW TO AVOID THE MARGINAL HOUSE AND GET A BETTER DEAL

How do you tell the difference between the marginal house and a really good house? It comes down to knowing the distinguishing traits of good-quality products and materials.

If you are buying a new house of marginal quality, as determined by inspection of the builder's model or blueprints, you simply request that the house being built for you contain better-quality materials. Give the builder a list of the changes you want. Most builders will accommodate you, though they will, of course, charge you for each change. If you think you are being overcharged, check the additional cost for the quality materials you want with the particular supplier involved; for example, a plumbing-supply house for bathroom-fixtures prices, a heating contractor for the cost of the best furnace, the lumberyard for building-materials prices, and so on.

You may also save money by having the builder omit certain features ordinarily included in the house, features you consider of small importance. The model house may contain a fancy intercom system, say, or a finished downstairs recreation room, or other such features usually included more for their initial sales appeal than for function. If they appeal little to you, consider trading them off for extra quality in the house. Your extra cost for the house will come down.

If you are considering an already-built new house that is of marginal quality, unfortunately there is little you can do about it. You can buy it as is, accepting its shortcomings, or pass it up. Sometimes, however, if you really like the house, a builder will build another one for you with the higher-quality standards you specifically request.

If you are considering a used house, obviously you can do little to change its construction quality. But by knowing about good-quality construction you can avoid the marginal house and aim for one that is well built.

■ WHAT ABOUT FHA QUALITY?

How much extra construction quality do you get if you buy an FHA house? That, of course, is a house that has been approved for an FHA mortgage. Consider first a new house that was approved for FHA financing before construction on the house began. Buying a new FHA house is a big step in the right direction. It means the house is built according to FHA's Minimum Property Standards. (But note again that word *minimum!*) Many parts of the house will be of higher-than-average quality, but by no means all. By and large, FHA's construction rules, its building standards, are stiffer and more uncompromising than any other building standards in effect for houses today. But they do not mean that you will get uniformly high quality throughout the house. The FHA rulebook covers hundreds of things in a house. Sad to say, not all of them are high-quality specifications. Some are written so that minimum quality will easily get by. You therefore must go a step further to avoid marginal quality even in an FHA house.

Suppose you are buying a used house with an FHA mortgage. You could still get a marginal house, although there is less likelihood of getting a defective house. An FHA inspector will check the house. Comparatively speaking, the FHA (and VA) inspections are quite thorough, but because of the nature of used houses, not only is a comprehensive structural evaluation impossible, but the quality of construction need meet only minimum standards. It could be a house of marginal quality and still get FHA (or VA) approval.

Ask an FHA lender for detailed information on FHA construction standards; knowing those standards can be helpful whether you're buying a new or used house, with or without an FHA mortgage.

■ THE HALLMARKS OF THE QUALITY HOUSE

Here is a summary of high-quality features to look for when you buy a house.

Foundation walls.   Foundation walls of poured concrete, also called cast-in-place walls, are usually better than concrete-block or cinder-block walls. Poured walls offer better natural waterproofing and are more durable and far more resistant to termites. The best quality requires a good cement mix. The use of one extra sack of cement per cubic yard, compared with the usual practices, can virtually ensure high-quality strength and permanence.

Concrete-block walls should be pargeted (plastered) with a 2 inch of cement mortar on the outside. Much extra strength is gained if they are also laced with joint reinforcement rods. These would be placed in the mortar beds between courses of block—generally every few courses.

Whichever type of foundation, ask for troweled-on waterproofing instead of the usual brush-on or spray-on type. If local water conditions are bad, protection can be further improved with a film of polyethylene or asphalt-impregnated membrane. Running this film right down to the base of the footing will seal all joints. Another good waterproofing material is bentonite clay panels placed against the foundation before backfilling.

A system of tile drainpipe should be put in the ground around the house at the base of the foundation walls, except in dry areas. This gets rid of groundwater that would otherwise get into the basement. It is often the only way to keep the basement dry. Insist on it if you want to avoid a wet basement.

Termite protection. Termite protection is recommended in nearly all states but Alaska. You can use either soil chemicals, chemically treated timber or termite shields. As noted before, a poured-concrete foundation will provide additional protection.

Exterior walls. Exterior walls should be rugged and durable, with a long-lasting finish. If the home is not brick, prefinished wall siding is highly recommended to reduce repainting. This includes prefinished hardboard or wood, vinyl or aluminum siding, galvanized steel, plywood, or mineral-fiber sidings. Such materials should have a name brand. The best kinds are guaranteed—the longer the guarantee, the better.

If the walls are painted, insist on top-of-the-line paint, the very best. It should be a well-known brand. Get a three-coat job—a primer and two finish coats. Make sure the siding is applied with double galvanized, aluminum or other rustproof nails. Be sure each nailhead is set below the surface of the wood and covered with putty. Also be sure that any joints between siding boards are puttied over and that all window and door trim is properly caulked with one of the new rubber-based caulking compounds that stay flexible.

Interior walls. Interior walls are usually made of 2-inch plasterboard today; it is basically satisfactory and better than the δ-inch plasterboard sometimes used. Even better is the ε-inch thickness. Best of all, particularly for superior sound control and a nail-free surface, is a two-layer wall in which one layer of δ-inch plaster-board is laminated over another. With either one- or two-layer walls, the builder should use three layers of compound over joints and nail-heads.

On paneled walls prefinished materials give easier cleaning, plus resistance to soiling, marring and stains. Wood paneling gains fire resistance if applied over plaster-board or asbestos-cement board instead of directly to the framing members. With plaster, two coats over metal lath is good; three coats is better, though rarely done today.

Flooring.   Flooring should be closely fitted and display no wide gaps and no high edges. That goes for hardwood strips or block as well as resilient flooring. No squeaks should be heard when you walk over it slowly. The appearance of hardwood flooring varies according to the wood used—oak and maple are the king and queen of the hardwoods—and also according to grade. For example, the highest-grade, finest-grained oak is "Clear," and it costs a few cents more per square foot than the second grade, "Select," which in turn runs about 3 to 5 cents more per square foot than "No. 1 Common." With wooden floors, ask for a top-grade polyurethane floor finish, which will glisten for a year or so without waxing.

Resilient flooring starts with asphalt tile, the cheapest and lowest quality; it's good for a concrete basement floor, but that's about all. Next in price comes asphalt asbestos tile, a questionable material in a hard-wear location and potentially hazardous because it might generate asbestos dust. Finally, there are pure vinyl, rubber and cork tiles. Pure vinyl is best for most uses. Rubber has only fair resistance to oil and grease. Cork can look exceedingly rich and handsome but will soon look worn in heavy-traffic rooms. There is also sheet linoleum, the granddaddy of composition flooring, which is cheap. It is easily damaged by water and is therefore not the best material for kitchens and bathrooms. Get the heaviest gauge available and definitely the "inlaid" kind; cut through a sample, and you should see that the grain goes all the way through from one surface to the other.

Windows and doors. Windows and doors should be a well-known national brand, such as Andersen and Pella. They should fit tightly, open and close easily, and be easy to clean from inside. Weather stripping should be built into the frames; you should see it. Aluminum windows should contain plastic fittings to prevent a direct connection (thus no cold flow) between the movable parts and the frame. The best kind come with provisions for easily slipping in a screen and a storm-glass panel. In a cold climate, double-glass windows (such as Thermopane or Twindow) can pay in better comfort, particularly in a new house, where they save the cost of storm windows. Double-glass windows will cost, all told, about 10 percent to 20 percent more than the combined cost of ordinary single-pane glass windows plus storm windows.

Kitchen countertop surfaces. Kitchen countertop surfaces should be a plastic laminate (Formica, Micarta or Panelite) or possibly ceramic tile that is even tougher, though it's hard on dropped chinaware. The best kitchen cabinets are those of a brand-name manufacturer with a rugged factory-applied finish. Steel cabinets should be heavy-gauge material (feel them in different houses).

There should be enough electrical outlets behind the countertop for plugging in small appliances, and one or two double outlets where the kitchen table will go. Overhead lighting should flood the length of the countertop; one light in the middle of the room is not enough.

Bathroom fixtures. Bathroom fixtures should all show the imprint of national manufacturers (Kohler, Moen, Elkay and Grohe are some). This is important because the same manufacturers do not stamp their name on their lowest-quality fixtures. An enameled cast-iron tub has the edge over the enameled steel tub. Cast iron is less apt to chip or wear and comes in more styles and sizes. Tall people who like to take tub baths should be sure the tub is long enough. They range in length from 6 feet long down to pygmy length. The depth inside will vary from 15¼ inches down to a shallow 12½

FIGURE 8.2 ■

Top-notch cabinetry makes this kitchen highly functional and attractive. The award-winning design is by Cathy Larsen-Jepson, CKD, CBD; Bolig Kitchen Studio. (*Photo courtesy of the National Kitchen & Bath Association [NKBA] from the NKBA Design Competition.*)

inches. You'll probably want the deepest kind, not only for baths, but also because it will mean less water splashing on the floor.

In new houses, rigid fiberglass and acrylic plastic lavatories, bathtubs and shower stalls are becoming more common. They can be very good, provided that you're getting well made ones. They are attractive, tough and long lasting; they're made of the same tough plastic used for boat hulls, which must withstand rugged exposure to water and hard knocks. Plastic units are also warm to the touch, a welcome comfort in winter. If you're buying a new house with plastic fixtures, specify a brand that meets the stiff design standards of the American National Standards Institute or ANSI Z 124, 1-1974. A shower unit should meet the ANSI Z 124, 2-1967 standard. Accept only a plastic lavatory made by a well-known company that will replace it if something goes wrong.

Flushing action is the key to toilet quality. Cheapest of all is a wash-down model, the poorest and the least sanitary. Next steps up in quality are: the reverse-trap action unit; the siphon jet, quite good; and the siphon-jet vortex, best of all and the kind used for the luxury one-piece quiet-flush toilets. The one-piece wall-mounted toilet makes cleaning the bathroom easier, though it has a luxury price tag. Whatever the toilet model, test it for noise and effectiveness by flushing it.

The best lavatory bowls are made of gleaming vitreous china. They are only slightly more expensive than enameled cast iron, which is next best. There are also enameled steel bowls, third in quality and more susceptible to chipping and wear.

When you judge the lavatory basin, think big. It should be large enough for comfortable use, especially if you use it for washing your hair or for bathing an infant. There are skimpy sizes as small as 15 inches × 17 inches, and large ones up to about 28 inches × 20 inches. Try for at least 20 inches × 24 inches; these cost only a few dollars more than the smallest ones.

Good faucets are made of solid brass with a tough coat of chrome, nickel, or brushed or polished brass. The marginal kinds are usually made of lightweight zinc or aluminum castings that tarnish quickly, drip and look dreadful within a short time. The cheapest kinds can often be identified by their crosslike handle, four horizontal spokes coming out from the center. The solid-brass kind generally has a solid handle with grooves for your fingers. Good faucets cost a little more but are worth it. They are made with a good water valve that does not have a rubber washer. Some manufacturers use a tough ceramic disk; others a hard plastic mechanism. If the valve seat goes bad, you merely replace it. A replaceable valve seat is a key feature to look for. Single-lever-control faucets are also available and good (one of the best brands is Moen); they offer ease of operation as well as good quality. This applies to the kitchen faucet as well as to those in bathrooms. There are also deluxe faucets, a third grade that offers little extra in quality. For a considerably greater cost, you get such luxury features as push-pull or dial control, or a monogrammed or Lucite handle.

The shower nozzle should have a flexible ball point for direction control and a spray control. These nozzles are self-cleaning. The cheap kind generally offers little or no control of direction or spray quality. Water, like energy, is becoming increasingly scarce and expensive, so a shower that doesn't waste water may be important. An adjustable nozzle with a rating of three to seven gallons a minute is usually satisfactory. An "automatic diverter control" should come with a combination shower-tub. It automatically diverts the water back to the tub faucets after someone has showered and so prevents the next person, who may want to take a tub bath, from being pelted with hot or cold water when turning on the faucets. Omission of the diverter, an inexpensive item, can also cause accidental scalding of children.

Bathroom accessories should include a large medicine cabinet, measuring at least 30 inches wide and 20 inches high. The doors should open easily. Other top-quality features are built-in linen closets, laundry hampers, a separate medicine cabinet with lock and key for safekeeping of pills and medicines that could harm children (a good place for it is high in the linen closet out of reach of kids), and good lighting, preferably with incandescent bulbs, because the usual fluorescent bulbs give a cold, harsh light that makes people look ghoulish.

Waterproof floors and walls, particularly around the tub and shower, are also essential. Ceramic tile is the old but proven wall and floor material, and you can hardly go wrong with it. It is not necessarily essential for the walls,

---

FIGURE 8.3 ■

This high-quality bathtub with brass plumbing fixtures and grip handles creates an elegant ambience in this prize-winning bathroom design by William Earnshaw, CKD, CBD; A & B Kitchen & Baths. (*Photo courtesy of the National Kitchen & Bath Association [NKBA] from the NKBA Design Competition.*)

except for the shower cubicle. There are also rugged new plastic wall materials, such as melamine-coated hardboard, that are very good. Not all are good, however, so if in doubt about the kind you see, check on its quality with a local tile supplier.

As for the flooring, avoid linoleum and asphalt tile in the bathroom. They quickly fall prey to water rot, and they are hard to keep clean and attractive. The flooring should be a tough pure vinyl or comparable material—ceramic tile or, say, marble or terrazzo.

Also check the bathroom for safety features such as grab bars in the shower (to prevent falls); a waterproof shower light; electric outlets well out of reach of the shower, tub and lavatory water (to prevent being electrocuted); and good quality soap holders and towel racks. Be sure there are shut-off valves at each fixture (so the water can be turned off for repairs without turning off the main water supply to the house).

Plumbing. Good plumbing starts even before the water meter. The water-supply pipe from the street to the meter should be at least ¾ to 1 inch in diameter, rather than the more usual ½ inch. That will ensure ample water pressure for the house. Copper pipe should be a must; it is now standard in many areas. Shutoff valves at every fixture are also a must. You should see them behind the kitchen sink as well as in the bathroom. An antiwater-hammer setup will cut down pipe pounding and also reduce faucet wear. Hot-water lines to distant bathrooms should either be insulated or have a hot-water recirculating line to provide instant hot water, particularly in winter.

Hot-water heater. The water heater, if fueled by gas or oil, should ordinarily have a tank capacity of 40 to 50 gallons, and be at least 80 gallons if electric, as noted in Chapter 7. In a new house, the kind of guarantee given on the water heater is the tip-off to quality. It should be guaranteed for at least 10 years; anything less is marginal.

If the water heater is an integral part of the hot-water boiler used for heating the house, minimum rating for a one-bath house is 2.75 gpm (gallons per minute of hot water); at least 3.25 gpm for two baths, more for a large family and large house. The rating will be on the boiler, and it also should have an IWH seal of good quality. That stands for an approved Indirect Water Heater. If there's no IWH seal, the quality is probably poor.

Septic system. A septic tank should have a capacity of at least 900 gallons for a three-bedroom house; 1,000 gallons

FIGURE 8.4 ■

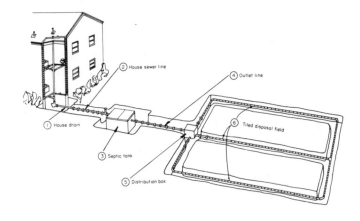

This shows how a septic-tank system for household sewer disposal is put underground. Find out the location of the septic tank when you buy a house so that it can be easily found for cleaning. (*All About Houses*)

for a four-bedroom; and at least 1,250 gallons for five or more bedrooms. It is best when the tank and its piping system (leaching field) are located in front of the house. That will facilitate the lowest-cost, most-direct connection to the sewer later. See Figure 8.4.

A percolation test is the real measure of septic-tank quality. This tells you how well the soil will absorb septic wastes and thus the size of the septic-tank system required. A test hole of 4 to 12 inches in diameter is dug in the ground, 2 inches of gravel is placed at the bottom, and at least 12 inches of water is poured over the gravel. The water is left standing for at least 4 hours and preferably overnight. The absorbing quality of the soil is determined by how long it takes for the water level to fall 1 inch. Properly carried out, the test will tell you whether or not a septic tank will work well and also how large a set of distribution pipes is required under the ground. The test should be carried out by an expert, preferably from the local health department. It is up to the homebuyer, however, to find out if the test was done and what the results were. It is important because many health experts estimate that in as many as 50 percent of all houses septic-tank systems do not work right.

Electrical system.   The electrical wiring should be supplied by a 240-volt three-wire feed from the telephone pole—you can actually see three wires—to a 240-volt electric board in the house. The main board should have a capacity of at least 100 amperes, but that's the absolute minimum recommended today. Look for a rating of 150 to 200 amperes noted on the board if electric heat is used or if it is a big house and you have a lot of electrical equipment. Inside the board there should be at least 15 to 20 individual circuit breakers (preferred over fuses) rather than a skimpy 8 or 10. There is one circuit breaker per wiring circuit. A board with extra circuits is very cheap if it is installed originally and much more expensive if you have to get one later.

■ ADDITIONAL FEATURES

The heavier asphalt roofing is, the longer it will last. Asphalt roof shingles of 235 pounds per "square" (one hundred square feet of shingling) in weight are the lightest you should accept. A superior grade is the "heavyweight" type, rated at 290 pounds per square, or better. They should be either the seal-down or the glue-tab kind to stay put on a roof in an area where violent windstorms or hurricanes occur.

Roof gutters and flashing of copper are traditionally noted for durability. Galvanized steel gutters are the usual kind and must be kept painted inside and out. They are better if they have a baked-on factory finish. Aluminum and vinyl gutters are even better.

The door hardware should be solid brass, solid bronze or solid aluminum. These materials are noted for long service; they also retain surface finish far longer than the usual iron or steel hardware that has a plated finish and may look solid but is not. Outside door locks should have a deadlock latch mechanism.

The attic should be fitted with appropriately sized air-vent louvers, not the small kind. These not only help cool the house in summer but also provide essential attic ventilation year round (to prevent condensation and wood-rot problems under the roof).

The Energy-Guzzler House

Poorly heated houses, beset with chilly drafts and cold rooms, were a problem in America even before energy prices soared. In 1965, for example, when home heating bills were comparatively low, a national survey found that "poor heating" was the second largest consumer complaint about American houses. (The number one complaint was "too small a house.") Heating a house satisfactorily, as well as economically, is important, just as the food you eat should be good as well as affordable.

Fortunately, many of the same things that keep energy bills down in winter help make a house warm and comfortable, too. Those things also make a house cooler in summer and reduce air-conditioning bills.

There are three main requirements for making a house warm in winter and cool in summer, as well as reducing its energy bills. They are (1) plenty of thermal insulation (including insulating window glass), the biggest single requirement; (2) proper exposure to the outdoor sun and cold (including design for natural solar heat entry in winter); and (3) new, high-efficiency heating equipment that by itself can cut winter heat bills as much as 40 percent, compared with the use of ordinary heating equipment.

FIGURE 9.1 ■

A well-designed house can combine the exciting outdoor vista provided by large glass walls and still be warm and comfortable indoors in winter, cool and quiet in summer. Double-thickness, insulating glass reduces cold entry indoors, and combination heating-cooling outlets, located in the floor directly under the glass, put up an additional fence of warm or cool air for indoor temperature control. (*Deck House, Inc., Acton, Mass.*)

This chapter tells how to obtain this threefold prescription for an energy-efficient house. It focuses largely on new houses because new houses set the standards for all houses and show you best how it's done. It also deals with making old houses energy efficient. By necessity, some parts that follow get a bit technical in order to provide essential facts for professional readers. Others may skip through such material.

A few facts about thermal comfort in houses should first be understood. There is more to being comfortable—meaning no chills, air drafts and goose-pimples indoors and fewer running noses and head colds—than heating and cooling per se. What's more, the same things that make a house cold and drafty in winter can also cause dry-air problems. The basic causes and cures for these problems and high energy bills are related.

■ WHAT MAKES PEOPLE COMFORTABLE?

True comfort in houses for most people requires an indoor temperature in winter of 72°F, give or take a degree or two, and relative humidity of 15 percent to 25 percent. These are proven conditions for indoor comfort, according to extensive physiological tests sponsored by the American Society of Heating, Refrigerating and Air-Conditioning Engineers, probably the foremost authority on the subject. Those conditions have been confirmed by actual experience in houses. If you must set your thermostat up to 75°F or higher, something is wrong, and you are spending too much money for heat.

■ INSULATION: TOP PRIORITY FOR COMFORT

The major cause of physical discomfort in a house is not poor heating, it is lack of insulation (see Figure 9.2). Even the best, most expensive heating system can't keep you warm if you've been shortchanged on insulation. With little or no insulation in winter, the exterior walls, floors and ceilings get quite cold. The heating thermostat can be turned up to 75°F or 80°F and the house air may be that hot, but it won't help much. The cold surrounding surfaces draw off excessive body heat from your skin by radiation. You get goose-pimples and feel chilled because body heat is drawn off faster than your blood can make it up. You feel cold for the same reason you feel chilled standing in front of an open refrigerator. The cold draws off too much body heat too fast. In addition, cold walls, windows and ceilings set up drafts that swirl into your rooms.

FIGURE 9.2 ■

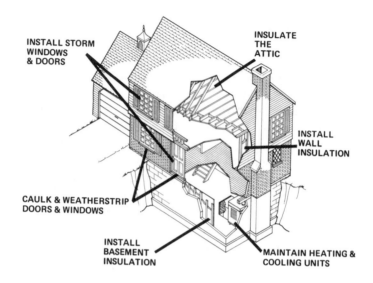

Here are the most important parts of a house, new or old, to conserve energy and keep down heating and cooling bills.

The cure is plenty of insulation. With thick insulation, the house shell and its interior surfaces do not get cold. Because they are warmer, body-heat loss to the surrounding house shell is reduced sharply. Cold drafts and little breezes do not swirl into the room. You're more comfortable at about 72°F. And the thermostat need not be raised way up. (This is a little-known reason why insulation contributes to lower fuel costs.)

Heat will always flow from a warm area to a cool area. This basic principle explains why a well-insulated home will keep you cooler on hot summer days and warmer in winter's chill. The effectiveness of insulation depends on its resistance to the flow of heat and is measured by R-value. The higher the R-value, the greater the insulating properties of the material. Of course, your requirements for insulation vary depending on your climate. Figure 9.3 will help you determine recommended insulation for an existing

FIGURE 9.3 ■

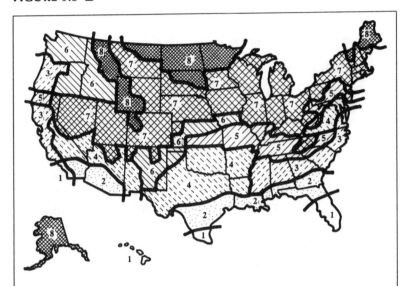

Recommended R-Values for Existing Houses in Eight Climate Zones

ZONE	Ceilings & Roofs		Floors over an Unheated Space		Exterior Wood Framed Walls		Crawlspace Walls	
	oil,gas, ht.pump	elect. resist.	oil,gas, ht.pump	elect. resist.	oil,gas, ht.pump	elect. resist.	oil,gas, ht.pump	elect. resist.
1	19	30	0	0	0	11	11	11
2	30	30	0	0	11	11	19	19
3	30	38	0	19	11	11	19	19
4	30	38	19	19	11	11	19	19
5	38	38	19	19	11	11	19	19
6	38	38	19	19	11	11	19	19
7	38	49	19	19	11	11	19	19
8	49	49	19	19	11	11	19	19

Thicknesses for Common Insulations to Obtain R-Values (Inches)

R-Value	Fiberglass Batts or Blanket	Blown-in Fiberglass	Blown-in Cellulose	Blown-in Rockwool	Polystyrene Foam (EPS)	(XPS)	Polyurethane-isocyanurate Foam
R-11	3.25-3.75	4.00-5.25	3.75	3.50	2.75	2.20	1.60-1.80
R-19	5.75-6.25	7.00-8.75	6.50	6.25	4.75	3.80	2.70-3.20
R-30	9.00-9.50	11.0-14.0	10.5	9.75	7.50	6.00	4.30-5.00
R-38	11.5-12.0	14.0-17.75	13.0	12.25	9.50	7.60	5.40-6.30
R-49	15.0-15.5	18.0-23.0	17.0	16.0	12.25	9.80	7.00-8.10

Data you can use to determine insulation requirements for your home based on climate conditions in your area of the United States (*Source: U.S. Department of Energy*)

house in your region. If you are buying a new home you may be able to do better.

The Superinsulated House

The School of Architecture-Building Research Council (BRC) at the University of Illinois has conducted research on approaches to designing and constructing houses for maximum conservation of energy. They called their model the Illinois Lo-Cal House. Their design included maximum insulation, multiple glazing and passive solar orientation. To measure the benefits of their design, the council built a test house and used scientific recording techniques and instrumentation in addition to computer modeling. The goal of the program was to develop a model energy-efficient home that used readily available building materials and required no unusual processes either for contractors or the occupants. In other words, it was to be replicable in the real world.

The most unique feature was a double-wall construction that allowed for continuous insulation (8½ inches throughout the wall), thus decreasing heat transfer through studs and headers. This design was used on three sides of the house. The south wall used a conventional 2 × 4 stud structure and 3½ inches of insulation. A continuous polyethylene vapor retarder was installed on the walls and ceiling, reducing air infiltration through the house. The floor insulation had an R-value of 20, and ceiling insulation had an R-value of 40. The danger of a highly insulated house is that there may not be enough air circulation. In this house the ventilation rate was below recommended levels, a problem the designers addressed by installing air-to-air heat exchangers.

Researchers measured the increase in energy use when certain insulation features were removed, a method that revealed the most benefical insulating features for a house. Windows can make a big difference. Going from triple-pane to double-pane windows increased energy use by just 9 percent. However, going to single pane increased it by 42 percent. Also, it is well worth it to insulate floors and ceilings.

Removal of floor insulation resulted in a 24 percent increase in energy use. When ceiling insulation was decreased by half, energy use increased by 19 percent; removing the ceiling insulation altogether caused a whopping 203 percent jump. Using a combined model of what would be a standard house, the researchers determined that their Lo-Cal model would use half the heating energy of a typical house. This has been confirmed by an actual occupant. Architect and owner of the research house, Michael T. McCulley, has commented that the house has been comfortable and economical in both summer and winter. "We have begun to take the low energy bills for granted and must periodically compare them to others' bills for conventional houses to appreciate having bills half to a third of those of other people in similarly sized houses," he commented after nine years of living in the house.

In sum, the superinsulated house in one fell swoop has made obsolete a number of other proposals for beating the high cost of home heating and cooling in houses. That includes such developments as the earth-sheltered house and mechanical solar heating with roof-top heat collectors, also called active solar heat. While this is a research model, not an actual house from a builder's lot, the results clearly demonstrate the benefits of superior insulating features in a house.

Detailed technical information on the project is available in a booklet entitled *Superinsulated House* (Research Report 86-1). In addition to technical reports, the BRC publishes many helpful and low-priced consumer pamphlets on house design and construction. If you are purchasing a new home and have some choice on the amount of insulation to use, you should look at the booklet *Saving by Insulating*, which contains worksheets to help you calculate how much money various levels of insulation can save you. You can phone 800-336-0616 for a listing of all BRC publications.

What's the Best Insulation?

The best kinds are polyurethane and polystyrene, both loosely called "foam" insulation (see Figure 9.4). They give you the best defense against heat loss per inch of thickness. In other words, they carry the highest R-values. They are expensive, though. They are therefore used chiefly for squeezing in maximum insulation for a house where space is limited, for wall sheathing (inner skin), a roof deck or in the foundation wall of a concrete-floor house.

Polyurethane and polystyrene are roughly 50 percent to 100 percent better than mineral-wool insulation, the third best all-around insulation for houses. In other words, an inch of urethane is roughly equivalent to 1½ inches to 2 inches of mineral wool.

Mineral-wool insulation, however, is more widely used because it's less expensive and it's versatile. Mineral wool is a generic term that includes fiberglass, glass wool and rock-wool insulation. These shine in houses because of relatively high R-values and because each is an inorganic material. That means rotproof, fire-resistant and unlikely to be eaten or turned into nests by bugs or mice. Mineral wool can be prickly, though. Installing it usually calls for hand gloves and a mask.

Other insulation for houses includes wood fiber and cellulose fiber. It is also called macerated paper and is made from old newsprint, perlite and vermiculite.

Wood-fiber and cellulose insulation are mainly "loose-fill" insulations—that is, they are poured from bags over an attic floor or blown into a wall cavity with a blower. Their big attraction is low price. But the low price is offset by high risk, and they cannot be fully recommended. Trouble can arise with wood fiber and cellulose because each is an organic material that requires chemical treatment for resistance to fire, bugs and rot. Some brands, however, are sold with poor chemical treatment, if any at all. They will rot, burn or attract rodents. As a result, a few bad apples have spoiled the barrel, and you can't be sure about the quality of wood fiber or cellulose.

FIGURE 9.4 ■ How Different Insulations Compare

Insulation	R-value per inch of thickness
Plastic foam, including polyurethane and polystyrene boards and sheets	3.8 to 6.3
Mineral wool, rock wool, fiberglass batts and blankets	3.2 to 3.7
Mineral wool, rock wool, fiberglass loose fill	2.2 to 3.0
Cellulose loose fill	3.2 to 3.7
Perlite	2.7
Vermiculite	2.2

To determine the R-value of insulation more than 1 inch thick, multiply the thickness by the R-value per inch. For example, 3 inches of a fiberglass batt with an R per inch of 3.3 will give you a total R-value of 9.9 (3 times 3.3).

Perlite and vermiculite are mineral kinds of loose insulation with relatively low performance (i.e., low R-values). They are easily poured over an attic floor or into a structural cavity where they can provide permanent protection at relatively low cost. Perlite is about 20 percent more effective than vermiculite, as shown in Figure 9.4; 5 inches of perlite will perform as well as 6 inches of vermiculite.

Vapor Barriers

Virtually every house should be lined with a vapor barrier to prevent moisture damage to the structure. A vapor barrier is a relatively impermeable material, such as aluminum foil or a black asphalt or brown paper cover integral with the insulation used, or it may be a polyethylene plastic sheet that lines the house shell. It usually goes between the insulation and the inside of the house. A vapor barrier is also essential under the concrete floor of a slab-on-ground house. There it is usually a large sheet of polyethylene plastic laid over the ground bed before the cement is poured.

That prevents groundwater vapor from rising up into the house where it could cause damage.

Insulated Doors and Windows

Triple-pane window glass is now considered essential for energy efficiency in a house. It can pay for itself in high comfort inside the house as well as savings on energy bills. At the very least, triple glass is recommended in a large house in a climate of 6,000 degree days or more. (Degree days is the way to measure the severity of winter, and in the United States varies from less than 1,000 in southern Florida to nearly 10,000 by the Canadian border.) Nothing less than double-pane glass windows should be acceptable in climates with 4,500 to 6,000 degree days. See Figure 9.5.

The insulated door is, surprisingly, relatively new in houses. Today in the North nearly every outside door should incorporate insulation. Omitting door insulation is almost as bad as leaving the door ajar.

■ SOLAR HEAT

Passive solar is the breed of solar heat that costs comparatively little money to install but can pay off with big dividends. It's pure sunshine pouring into a house through window glass. A small area of glass can let in a huge amount of heat. Consider an average day in January. Enough sun can pour into the average-size American home (1,600 square feet) in the North through a mere 35 square feet of glass facing south to heat the whole house for 24 hours! That's solar impact.

More than that minimal area of glass is often used to allow for winter days with partial sunshine. The house need not face due south. Up to 30° east or west of south is all right.

There are two ways to use solar heat. We'll call them Plan A and Plan B. Plan A is easier and cheaper but less efficient. It's merely putting a lot of window glass on the south

FIGURE 9.5 ■

Classic photograph shows how double-pane insulating glass (left) does not frost up in winter. Twindow glass is used here. Glass at right is ordinary single-pane glass. (*Pittsburgh Plate Glass Company*)

side of your house and letting the winter sun shine in during the day. This was done with the Illinois BRC superinsulated house. It's also done in many actual houses, sometimes with a solarium or with a simple sunroom design. Vents or ducts are installed to distribute the captured heat to other parts of the house. At night, thermal shades can be drawn down over the glass to conserve interior heat. Or the room can be closed off from the rest of the house.

Windows made with double- or triple-pane glass can also reduce heat leakage from a house (see Figure 9.6 and Figure 9.7). By the way, multipane window glass lets just as much solar heat enter a house as single-pane glass, but

FIGURE 9.6 ■

Double-pane, high-efficiency glass can cut heat loss from a house in winter by up to 50 percent. In summer it can reduce heat entry by 41 percent, hence lower energy bills year round. (*Photo of Andersen® High Performance™ insulating glass courtesy of Andersen Windows, Inc.*)

multipane sharply cuts the flow of house heat going out because that heat travels in a different way through glass.

The next step up, Plan B, uses much more of the captured sunshine to heat a house. It's the ultimate passive solar heat, providing as much as 60 percent of the home heat needed. It's called passive solar. Active solar uses roof collectors, pipes, pumps and other active machinery.

The trick with passive solar, Plan B, is spreading the trapped heat efficiently throughout the house by planned air circulation and by storing the surplus heat caught so it

FIGURE 9.7 ■

An insulated window on the southern wall, along with orientation or exterior design that provides shade in the summertime, is the simplest passive solar design feature. These glass doors and arched windows add a feeling of spaciousness to the room and contribute to the enjoyment of the outdoors. (*Photo courtesy of Andersen Windows, Inc.*)

can warm the house at night. A solar house must also be very well insulated so that little heat can leak out. Storing the daytime heat is, so far, done with concrete or slate flooring, with canisters of special chemicals and even with barrels of water that are attractively built into the house. Each is heated up by the sun during the day and slowly releases its heat indoors at night.

These and other heat-storage methods are, alas, largely experimental at this time. Some appear to be working well, but issuing a final report on them may take time.

As for mechanical or active solar heat, we believe that this simply cannot be recommended for houses today. To review: it can be quite expensive, it's still unproven and it's seldom, if ever, guaranteed. Besides, a superinsulated house can provide A-plus interior warmth and comfort, more efficient heating and even larger energy savings for considerably less money.

■ TOP-NOTCH NEW HEATING

Introduced in 1982, new high-efficiency (HE) heating units can cut gas and oil fuel bills in houses by 25 percent to 40 percent, compared with conventional home heaters that were used in most houses in the United States. Among other features, the new heaters do not require a chimney (only a small exhaust vent to outdoors), and they use electronic ignition (hence no pilot light burning all the time). They are as much of an advance in home heating as the jet plane was over the propeller plane.

Their high performance is the result of their ability to extract 90 percent to 95 percent of the heat content from every unit of fuel burned. The gas and oil home heaters in most houses extract only 60 percent to 75 percent of the heat from the fuel they burn. The rest goes up the chimney. Federal energy regulations implemented in 1992 require new furnaces and boilers to have an efficiency rating of 78 percent or higher.

The new HE units are called recuperative or condensing heating units. They incorporate a special coil that recoups most of the heat that would otherwise go up the chimney. They're also called condensing heating units because a good portion of the flue heat is extracted from hot water vapor condensing out of the flue gases.

Some new home heaters on the market are called HE units, but they are not. They should have a recuperative or condensing coil; so far, that is the only kind of home heating unit with truly high efficiency.

Another check for a true HE unit is to be sure that one you get doesn't require a chimney; if it does it's not the real thing. A house chimney is needed chiefly for fire protection from the high temperature flue gases of about 500°F, or less.

That's a lot of wasted heat. Because much of that heat is recouped from the flue gases, the temperature of the flue fumes from a new HE heater is reduced to as low as 100°F and a chimney is no longer needed. The flue gases are vented outdoors through the nearest wall.

Gas versus Oil Heat

Which is cheaper? Which is better? With few exceptions, gas heat is generally cheaper to buy and operate and is usually better than oil for home heating. Gas heat is generally cleaner, simpler to use and requires less service and maintenance. Gas costs less to install in part because it does not need the tank needed for oil heat. Natural gas is, of course, piped into a house with no tank needed, with one exception. That's when bottled liquefied propane (LP) gas is used, requiring a storage tank.

Choosing Low-Cost Heat Energy

How do gas, oil and electric heat bills compare with each other? It depends on the price of each where you live. Gas and electric costs vary from one part of the country to another. Gas is usually cheapest in the South and Southwest, near the great underground gas fields. Its cost rises in other areas largely because of distribution costs. Electric rates vary from area to area for other reasons. The price of oil is largely uniform throughout the country.

The relative cost of oil, gas and electricity can be obtained from Figure 9.8, a comparison table on energy. There are three columns under electricity based on a heat pump rating system called Coefficiency of Performance (COP). Electricity resistance, described later in the chapter, has a COP of 1. The average air-to-air heat pump in the Midwest has a COP of 2. A geothermal heat pump has an average COP of 3.5. Listings are also shown for 80 percent and 93 percent efficiency furnaces or boilers running on gas, propane or oil. For example, suppose that the price of natural gas where you live is 82 cents a therm (100,000 Btu's of energy). The table shows that that's equivalent to heating with oil at roughly $1.15 a gallon and electricity resistance at 3.5 cents per kilowatt-hour. If oil and electricity cost more in your area, gas heating is cheaper. The higher the price of each, the higher your bill in comparison with gas, and the more you save with gas heating.

Gas and electricity costs generally fall on a sliding scale. The more you use, the lower the unit price. Thus, gas and electricity are cheaper for house heat than when used only for kitchen purposes. Get the cost of each from a knowledgeable heating expert or an engineer at your local gas or electric company. Ask them how the costs of gas, oil and electricity compare for home heating. A straight answer generally will be obtained from a utility company expert, though some will, of course, shade it in their favor. For a new house, an estimate of annual heating costs with gas and electricity can also be obtained from many utility companies.

■ WHAT KIND OF HEATING SYSTEM?

The three main kinds of central heat in houses today are warm-air heat, the most widely used; hot-water, also called hydronic heat; and electric heat. Each can perform very well provided good equipment is used and it is installed properly.

Forced Warm-Air Heat

Consider warm-air heating first. Technically, it is forced warm-air heat because a blower sends heated air through ducts to the rooms of your house. It is often referred to simply as forced air. The blower and the air ducts are its telltale signs.

Forced warm-air heat has become dominant in the United States because it's less costly to install than hot-water heat, and it can be economically coupled with central air-conditioning in a house; the same air ducts are used for

FIGURE 9.8 ■ Relative Cost of Heating Fuels

Electricity COP			Natural Gas Seasonal Efficiency		Propane Seasonal Efficency		Oil Seasonal Efficiency	
1	2	3.5	80%	93%	80%	93%	80%	93%
1.5¢	3.0¢	5.3¢	$0.35	$0.41	$0.32	$0.38	$0.49	$0.57
1.8¢	3.5¢	6.1¢	$0.41	$0.48	$0.38	$0.44	$0.57	$0.67
2.0¢	4.0¢	7.0¢	$0.47	$0.55	$0.43	$0.50	$0.66	$0.76
2.3¢	4.5¢	7.9¢	$0.53	$0.61	$0.49	$0.56	$0.74	$0.86
2.5¢	5.0¢	8.8¢	$0.59	$0.68	$0.54	$0.63	$0.82	$0.95
2.8¢	5.5¢	9.6¢	$0.64	$0.75	$0.59	$0.69	$0.90	$1.05
3.0¢	6.0¢	10.5¢	$0.70	$0.82	$0.65	$0.75	$0.98	$1.14
3.3¢	6.5¢	11.4¢	$0.76	$0.89	$0.70	$0.81	$1.07	$1.24
3.5¢	7.0¢	12.3¢	$0.82	$0.95	$0.75	$0.88	$1.15	$1.34
3.8¢	7.5¢	13.1¢	$0.88	$1.02	$0.81	$0.94	$1.23	$1.43
4.0¢	8.0¢	14.0¢	$0.94	$1.09	$0.86	$1.00	$1.31	$1.53
4.3¢	8.5¢	14.9¢	$1.00	$1.16	$0.92	$1.07	$1.40	$1.62
4.5¢	9.0¢	15.8¢	$1.06	$1.23	$0.97	$1.13	$1.48	$1.72
4.8¢	9.5¢	16.6¢	$1.11	$1.29	$1.02	$1.19	$1.56	$1.81
5.0¢	10.0¢	17.5¢	$1.17	$1.36	$1.08	$1.25	$1.64	$1.91
5.3¢	10.5¢	18.4¢	$1.23	$1.43	$1.13	$1.32	$1.72	$2.00
5.5¢	11.0¢	19.3¢	$1.29	$1.50	$1.19	$1.38	$1.81	$2.10
5.8¢	11.5¢	20.1¢	$1.35	$1.57	$1.24	$1.44	$1.89	$2.19
6.0¢	12.0¢	21.0¢	$1.41	$1.64	$1.29	$1.50	$1.97	$2.29

Source: U of I Building Research Council "Heating the Home." Reprinted with permission.

heating and cooling. Adding air ducts just for air-conditioning to a house with hot-water or electric heat can get expensive. In addition, warm air, with its air circulation feature, can be a decided plus factor in a house with passive solar heat. As noted earlier, it can circulate trapped solar heat throughout the house.

The quality of a warm-air system depends on the kind of furnace and how well the vital ducts are designed. Look for a furnace with a 10-year warranty (on its combustion

chamber) and a pulley-driven blower. This is the better custom kind, costing only a little more than the marginal
builder or "economy" kind. Take off the front panel and see
if the blower is driven by a rubber pulley, like an automobile fan belt. It connects the blower to the electric motor that
drives it. If there is no pulley and the blower is connected
directly to its motor—same shaft for both—it is almost
always the sign of a low-price economy furnace with a one-
year warranty only. Don't go by the brand because even the
best manufacturers sell both kinds.

The duct system, crucial for good heat supply and uniform temperatures, should be what engineers call a perimeter design. The warm-air outlets in the rooms should be
located in the floor or at wall baseboard level. And most
important, they should be located in the outside-facing
walls of the house, preferably under windows, in order to
supply the heat at the source of the greatest cold—the exterior walls and windows. Usually at least one outlet should
be located at each exterior wall in a room. Two or more are
often needed in large rooms or along extended walls under
long picture windows. A curtain of warm air should be
thrown up from the registers around the house between you
and the outside cold.

Perimeter heating is usually essential for good heating
in a cold climate, especially in a house with no basement. It
is less important in a warm climate. The warm-air system
that often causes problems is one with the supply outlets,
the registers, located in the interior walls or at ceiling level.
This design, by and large, works well only in a mild winter
climate with one exception. That's in a superinsulated
house where perimeter heat supply may not be essential for
comfort. A simple, less expensive air-circulation system
could provide highly satisfactory heating comfort in a house
where cold drafts and chills are not likely as a result the
superinsulation.

If a house has two or more floor levels or is a long,
spread-out ranch, it should generally have separate heating
zones. This calls for two or more thermostats, each providing custom heat control for each zone. That's how to get

uniform temperature control and prevent some rooms from getting too hot while others are too cold. Zone controls are also good for many houses with hot-water heat.

Hot-Water (Hydronic) Heat

Water is heated in a central boiler and flows to room radiators. The best kind is a forced circulating system that has a pump to push the water around. There are cast-iron and steel boilers. A cast-iron one is far more rugged and dependable and is usually guaranteed for at least 20 years. Naturally it costs more than a steel boiler. It should show an IBR seal on its nameplate, which means it conforms with the design standards of the Institute of Boiler and Radiator Manufacturers.

A steel boiler can be adequate in an area with soft water; but if your water supply is hard and corrosive, steel should be shunned like the plague. A good steel boiler will display on its nameplate an SBI seal (Steel Boiler Institute).

There should be enough radiators around the exterior walls. What is enough? This varies from house to house. There are no set rules. Do look for at least one radiator below each exposed wall of a room, and more than one for long wall exposures.

The best radiators are the long, low, baseboard kind, about 6 to 10 inches high and up to 10 feet or so long. They are usually made with copper or aluminum heating fins. They are sometimes difficult to clean, though, and may be noisy when the heat goes on and off. There are also cast-iron baseboard radiators, the A-plus kind. But they are expensive and you will generally see them only in the best houses.

If a house has hot-water radiant floor heat, tread warily. Hot water circulates through pipes embedded in the floor, usually of concrete, and the floor acts as a heating panel for the house, like a low-temperature hot plate. There are some perfectly good radiant systems, but unfortunately there are many poor ones because they are hard to design and install properly. If a pipe breaks, the floor has to be dug up. Another drawback of radiant heat is sluggish operation. The whole floor has to heat up before you get heat, and that can take an hour or two. It's best to avoid radiant heat unless you are assured that it has been properly installed.

Electric Heat

Two crucial prerequisites for efficient electric heat are a very well insulated house and a local electric rate that is low enough to make it feasible. If keeping your monthly heating bills down is important, don't compromise on these needs.

Because electric rates can be high, getting the estimated electric heating bill for a new house from the electric company is a wise thing to do. To confirm the figures, check the actual operating costs of other people nearby with electric heat. In a used house with electric heat there's a virtually unbeatable way to determine the heating cost—see the owner's actual heating bills, or ask permission to obtain the bills from the electric company.

Electric heat has undeniable advantages: no fuel burned; no furnace or boiler to service, repair or replace; individual thermostats for each room (optional); and the lowest initial installation cost. As a result, you may be willing to pay a little more for its operation. You may like it even if the local electric rate runs high.

Be a little wary of electric heat in a new house. Some builders use it chiefly because of the low initial cost, even though local power rates are higher than they should be for economical operation. So be sure to get an estimate of its cost from the electric company.

When you check an installation, each of the electric-heat room radiators (convectors) should carry the UL seal of the Underwriters Laboratories. The system should be installed according to the standards of the National Electrical Manufacturers Association. Your contract for a new house should say this. If baseboard heating convectors are used, look for medium-density models, rated good, or low-density ones, the best. The high-density kind are the lowest in quality and performance. The best electric convectors will display the UL seal of the Underwriters Laboratory.

Is the Heating System Large Enough?

The heating system should be guaranteed to maintain 70°F or better in a house when the temperature outdoors is coldest in winter.

In Chicago that means –5°F outdoors; in New York, 0°F. In International Falls, Minnesota—one of our very coldest cities— –30°F is the outside temperature that a house heating system should be designed to cope with.

The heating capacity required for a superinsulated house in an average northern climate will be approximately 15 Btu's per square foot of living area. A superinsulated 2,000-square-foot house will therefore require a heating unit with 30,000 Btu's an hour of capacity. That will maintain 70°F in the house in a climate like that of New York City when it's 0°F outdoors, the coldest winter day usually experienced in those cities.

A similar house with fairly good but not super insulation and, say, double-pane rather than triple-pane windows, in the same climate will require a heating capacity of about 20 to 25 Btu's per square foot of area. That calls for heating with a capacity of up to 50,000 Btu's an hour. The heating capacity of a house heater should be marked in Btu's per hour on its nameplate.

That 50,000 Btu's an hour is roughly half of the heating capacity required for houses with ordinary insulation built prior to 1974, or in the days before the energy crunch. Most old houses required heating with a capacity of at least 50 Btu's per square foot of area; thus 100,000 Btu's of capacity for a 2,000-square-foot house. That much or more heating capacity is required in many old houses today with little or no insulation. No wonder many homeowners pay jumbo-size heating bills. They have energy-guzzler houses.

■ SUMMER COMFORT AND AIR-CONDITIONING

No question about it, in a hot summer climate central air-conditioning is essential for true comfort. It is no longer a luxury. It is also considered essential for house resale value in many parts of the country.

Air-conditioning has come on in the late 1900s much like the advent of central heat did around the turn of the twentieth century, and it promises to influence the way houses are built and the way we live as much in its way as central heat did. Any skeptic who doubts this should go back to the records of the early 1900s when central heat was kicking up a controversy. In 1906, a well-known women's magazine of the time (still a major magazine) blasted that newfangled device, the whole-house furnace, "with its forbidding installation cost." It cried that the potbellied coal stove was as fine a room heater as anyone could ask for. (The same magazine was also skeptical of another newcomer in houses, electricity, and cautioned its readers that "electricity is convenient but gaslight is still the best buy at seven times less cost.")

The installation cost of central air-conditioning is less than many people think, especially for a new house. Its cost in a superinsulated house is, like central heating, particularly low because of the low air-conditioning capacity required.

Central Air-Conditioning versus Single-Room Coolers

Installing window or through-the-wall air conditioners in a new house instead of central air-conditioning is no more recommended than adding single-room heating units rather than central heat for heating a house.

Central air-conditioning may cost more to install than single-room coolers (because of its ductwork). But the central unit is far more efficient, producing lower operating bills, is more reliable and will last longer. Besides, multiple room coolers are not only unattractive sticking out of a house, but they are also noisy.

Future Cooling Insurance

Understandably, central air-conditioning may be omitted from a new house because of its expense. But if you want it later, planning for it ahead of time could save considerable expense later. That's because the cost of adding central air-conditioning to a house after it's built is usually sharply higher than its installation cost in a new house being built. The need to alter the existing heating, break through walls, and so on, boosts the cost. Expensive future work can be neatly reduced by having a few low-cost provisions for the future air-conditioning installed while the house is being built.

First, this calls for central warm-air heating with air ducts. But have the builder and heating contractor install heating ducts that will accommodate central air-conditioning, too. Cooling usually requires bigger ducts. The furnace chosen should be one with a blower large enough for cooling; it also should be able to accommodate air-conditioning. Some automatically are, others are not. A special compartment (plenum) should be provided, usually above the furnace, where the cooling coil can be inserted at the proper time. The electrical wiring board should have provisions for a spare 240-volt circuit to handle the future air conditioner. If the supply air ducts pass through a room or space that will not be air-conditioned, like the garage or a crawl space, the ducts require insulation. Ducts in the basement, however, ordinarily need not be insulated for air-conditioning. These stitch-in-time provisions for cooling cost a relatively small extra sum when the house is being built, just as enlarging a closet or two ordinarily is not a big deal. That small extra expense spent in the beginning can save a substantial amount for adding central air-conditioning after the house is built. The extra cost during construction is good insurance.

How Much Air-Conditioning?

If air-conditioning is already in a new or an old house you may buy, is there enough for the house? It should be guaranteed to maintain the house at 75°F and 5 percent relative humidity indoors when the outside weather is at its worst. That means an outdoor design temperature of 95°F in northern cities like New York and Chicago, and 95°F also in certain southern cities like Houston, New Orleans and Miami. It may get more muggy and humid in those southern cities, but not necessarily hotter. In other southern cities, like Tulsa, Dallas and Phoenix, the outdoor design temperature in summer ranges from 100°F to 105°F. Thus, larger cooling units are required to keep a house at 75°F.

The Heat Pump

The heat pump is a summer-winter air conditioner, a device that supplies warm or cool air to a house with a refrigeration compressor. It has two coils, one indoors and one outdoors, and uses electricity to transfer heat between the coils. In summer it works like a regular air conditioner, removing heat from the house and dumping it outdoors. In winter the cycle is reversed, and it extracts heat from the outside air and delivers it inside. It is a form of electric heat. A house with a heat pump should, like a house with electric heat, be well insulated. And the size of your heating bills depends on the local cost of household electricity.

The cost of heating a house with a heat pump, however, is 25 percent to 50 percent less than the cost of regular electric resistance heating. The heat pump is more efficient because it extracts heat from the outdoor heat. That makes it a better bet than regular electric heat, especially in a house with central air-conditioning.

A heat pump saves the most money on heating in a comparatively mild northern climate, like that of Washington, D.C., where the winter temperature seldom drops below 15°F. The colder the climate, the less heat bonus compared with regular electric heat. This has to do with what's

called a heat pump's "balance point," the outdoor temperature at which a heat pump can no longer extract heat from
outdoor air. To continue heating a house when the air is
colder, a backup electric resistance heater is used with the
heat pump; it switches on to provide heat. Its operating cost
is naturally the same as regular electric heat. Heat-pump
balance points vary from brand to brand. The lower the balance point, the higher the efficiency. It can vary from about
30°F to 40°F, depending on the heat pump.

Compared with other heat, the operating bills with a
heat pump can run about twice as high as with oil heat and
three times as high as gas heat in the same house. The lower
the electric rate, the more competitive the heat pump. Its use
makes sense in areas where natural gas is high priced or
unavailable or where the electric rate is comparatively low.

One of the most efficient heating systems available
today is the geothermal heat pump that uses the earth's stable temperature. Vertical or horizontal pipes are buried at
least 5 feet below the surface, where the temperature is a
nearly constant 55°F. Installation is more expensive than the
traditional air-to-air heat pumps. The COP of a geothermal
system can be around 3.0 to 3.5.

Shop carefully for a good heat pump. Choose a type and
brand with a good performance record; among other things,
that means one that has been on the market for a year or
two, so the bugs have been eliminated. Choose one with an
energy efficiency ratio (EER) of at least 7.5. That's its summer operating efficiency. The higher it is, the better. The
unit's COP should range from about 2.0 at 15°F to 20°F, up
to 2.8 at 45°F to 50°F. That's a measure of winter heating efficiency.

■ CHECKING A USED HOUSE FOR ENERGY EFFICIENCY

Is the used house well insulated? Does it have a good
heating system? These are the two main requirements for
energy efficiency, as they are for a new house. In addition,

do the house and its main living areas and window glass face south? If so, that's a welcome bonus, as in a new house. If the house was clearly designed for passive solar heat, it's a decided extra bonus.

A used house for sale can be judged against the standards for new houses cited earlier, though few will meet the same high standards. The Department of Energy is preparing guidelines for a voluntary home energy rating system that should provide a basis of comparison, as does the miles-per-gallon rating of cars. The question is whether a used house will be energy efficient to a reasonable degree so that living in it won't exact a high price from you in discomfort and high fuel bills. Or how much money will be required to make the house sufficiently energy efficient for you?

Some used houses, of course, can be highly energy efficient. This includes the relatively new house built to high thermal standards that is for resale at a young age or the old house whose owner has thoroughly beefed-up the energy efficiency of his house. A highly energy-efficient used house like that can be worth a premium price, or as much as $5,000 to $10,000 more than a similar house with poor energy efficiency.

Paying that much more for an energy-efficient house could save you $500 to $1,000 a year, if not more. That's an annual return on your investment of 10 percent a year after taxes! That could be better than municipal bonds.

Checking for Insulation

Look for insulation at the attic floor over the ceiling, for double-pane glass or storm windows and doors, and for weatherstripping in good condition at the windows and doors. Determining if there's insulation in the walls can be difficult. The older the house, the less likely that wall insulation is present unless the owner had it pumped into the walls. Remove a few electric outlet covers and peer in with a flashlight. Can you see insulation? In cold weather the presence of drafts inside the walls is a tipoff to little or no wall insulation. In cold weather, also try the palm test. Put the palm of your hand flat against the inside surface of the exterior walls in several rooms. The walls should feel almost as warm to the touch as an interior wall in the middle of the house. If the outside wall is cold or downright chilly to the touch, there's little or no insulation.

The acid test is what the house heating bills are. Requesting the seller to produce them is now customary. What is the average total cost to heat the house each year? A request for summer air-conditioning bills is also recommended.

Unless you're an expert, hiring a good home inspection consultant is the best way to evaluate the heating system, as well as the insulation and the whole house.

A key question is how much money is required to make a house you buy sufficiently energy efficient for your needs and pocketbook. The most expensive work, if needed, is insulating the existing walls of a house, installing new storm windows and doors, and modernizing the heating system, not necessarily in that order. For typical used houses, one or more of these can cost from a few thousand dollars up to $10,000 and possibly more for a large house. Determining a more specific figure obviously requires obtaining estimates for a particular house from contractors. Obtaining such estimates can also serve as a basis for negotiating a lower price for the house to offset the cost of the improvements needed.

■ ═══CHAPTER 10═══ ■

The Gimmick House

A young couple bought a colonial house in a new development we'll call Highway Acres. But why did they buy that particular house in that particular development?

They bought it, of all things, principally because of a luminous Japanese ceiling in the downstairs bathroom. It was a distinctive, eye-catching feature, a suspended light screen illuminated by recessed lights above. What's more, it turned out later that more than half of the buyers of the 80 houses in Highway Acres also bought their houses largely because of the luminous ceiling feature in the one bathroom.

That's not unique, either. Surveys show that many houses are bought because of one or more distinctive features that trigger the buying impulse. The trouble is that such features are sometimes gimmicks, put there deliberately to catch the eye of buyers, in the same way that tail fins a few years ago were designed to sell cars (which they did by the millions), and eye-catching new packaging gimmicks flooding supermarket shelves are designed to trigger the buying impulse.

■ WHAT IS A GIMMICK HOUSE?

There's nothing basically wrong with manufacturers putting their best feet forward and making their products distinctive and attractive, thus more salable. But what is culpable are the gimmicks used to trick us into buying a product that is made to appear better than it actually is. The dictionary defines the word "gimmick" as "an attention-catching device, a novel twist, or a gadget. . . ."

Borrowing from that definition, we call the gimmick house a house with one or more special features that seem to make the whole house special, though this is not necessarily so. The houses in Highway Acres are marginal house traps, as many a buyer there has since found out. Measured against any real standards, they are of very poor design. The interior floor plan in most is a nightmare for living. The kitchens are singularly small and badly planned, and the construction is of marginal if not of downright shoddy quality. Yet the irresistible appeal of the Japanese ceiling so overshadowed the flaws that the builder sold some $2 million worth of marginal houses with the help of glamour ceilings at an extra cost of about $65 per house, not a bad investment.

Why did the Japanese ceiling trigger so many buying impulses? We don't know for sure, but what we were told may be a large part of the answer (as well as shedding light on how to avoid the gimmick-house trap). One of the buyers and present owners told us, "The ceiling was distinctive. My wife and I liked it at once. We liked the Japanese styling. Most of all, I think, it gave us confidence in the house. We felt that if the builder put something extra like that into the house, he probably took pains with the rest of the house. It made us feel that the whole house was especially well built."

The gimmicks used to sell houses take a variety of shapes and forms. They include fancy kitchen trappings like a dining-room pass-through wall, a shiny new wall oven, or an appliance plug-in center—all, in themselves, desirable additions—showy fireplaces, wrought-iron balcony rails, spiral staircases, roof pagodas, and so on. On a broader scale, there are also design gimmicks, such as the "raised ranch," the "Colonial ranch," and the "split ranch." There has also been the "atrium house," a house with an interior court (a splendid plan if carried off well). Each of these is a gimmick when it is built principally to sell the house irrespective of how well the house itself is designed and built.

To be sure, gimmicks can sometimes be perfectly functional and nice to have. The gimmick house is a trap to avoid, however, when one or two eye-catching features propel an unsuspecting couple into buying a house that they otherwise would not touch with a 10-foot pole. Are the house and its overall design and construction good, and is the house right for you and your family? Those are the key questions.

■ HOMEBUYING MOTIVATIONS

The subject of the gimmick house also raises an important question: Why do people buy houses? More to the point, why do people buy a particular kind of house? Certain strong emotional forces come into play when people buy houses. Much is still unknown about our motivations, though various studies have been made to find out. What has been learned can be instructive in defining your reasons for buying a house, as well as in helping you avoid the gimmick-house trap. Builders and real estate brokers continually search for the answers in order to find out how to sell more houses. It's time the homebuyer understood some of the forces at work, too!

Ask typical homebuyers why they seek a new house, and according to the usual superficial studies, they'll say they want more living space and bigger and better living quarters. Others want a little property of their own. But such reasons are only the beginning. According to a study by Cornell University researchers, some people buy houses chiefly for status and prestige reasons.

Others buy a house chiefly because it's a financial investment that will grow in value. Still other people most of all want a house that will best fulfill the personal needs of their families, with special emphasis on benefits for growing children (such as ample playing space and a location near good schools).

Scratch a little more, however, and we also learn that our houses tap wells of deep personal and psychological meaning to people. For instance, most of us have known persons who take great pride in their homes. Many people begin thinking of the decorating potential from the moment they first walk into a house for sale. Some people are less concerned with construction features. Others are far more concerned with the value of a house in terms of the kind of home it will be for themselves and their families.

Many people will walk down in the basement and check the furnace, climb into the attic for a look around and peer into corners to size up the kind of 2 x 4s used, even though they don't know the difference between a furnace and a boiler or between No. 1 clear hardwood and ordinary hardboard.

Many a person is also sharply motivated by the financial aspects of a house and such things as its resale value. Once a house is purchased, some derive great pleasure checking to see what other homes are selling for. That, too, is understandable.

There is also the person who cannot bear the emotional burden of a mortgage, cannot face up to buying and owning a house. Renting is much easier, even though buying and owning is almost always cheaper. The spouse usually wants to own a home. But one partner requires great and long persuasion to break through the emotional block and finally consent to buying a house. Sometimes it never works. One woman reported, "It took us four months to buy a house once we started looking. But first it took me seven years to talk my husband into it!"

■ NEW VERSUS OLD HOUSES

Surveys show that homebuyers belong in two categories—those who prefer new houses and those who prefer the old. People who seek a new house place great importance on having a house that is new and up-to-date. They are quoted in surveys as saying, "We want a place that is modern, new and clean." These words crop up in interviews again and again.

In the 1950s the ranch house was the newest style in houses, and as a result it was bought by the hundreds of thousands, if not by the millions. Then came the era of the split-level house. Split-levels were bought by droves of homebuyers because they were new and different, regardless of how well, or how badly, they were designed and built. Since then we have noted the introduction of houses like the split-entry, the raised ranch and the atrium house. Builders know that each holds irresistible appeal to many homebuyers, because each is supposed to be the very latest fashion in houses. Some people apparently do not realize that there are good atriums and bad ones, and just because a house is a new style doesn't mean that it is an especially good house.

Another study of homebuyers in a midwestern suburb showed that the kind of house was irrelevant as long as it was located in an area of new houses. This is particularly true for many young married people. They seek houses in a large new development, because they want to live among other young couples like themselves. They want to live where they can easily make friends with neighbors who are also starting out in life with common interests and young children like themselves. They fear, subconsciously perhaps, that buying a house in an older, established neighborhood would confront them with a difficult social situation. They are afraid, often rightly, that they and their children would be socially snubbed by the long-time neighbors around. It would be harder to make friends. They therefore head for new developments where everybody is starting out. The type of house is of secondary concern.

People who seek old houses do so for different reasons, too. Many are attracted to old houses by emotional forces as strong as those in people who seek new houses. They include persons who are, to be blunt, people who would not be caught dead in a new house development (but are sometimes caught financially dead by an old-house lemon). It includes others who have an honest wish for an old house with charm and tradition, sometimes because of their happy memories of growing up in a splendid old house. They like established communities filled with big trees and close to schools, shopping and commuter trains. They want to repeat the pleasure they had with their parents, doing it again with their children. Still others seek social and/or business prestige that they feel they can obtain only by buying a large old house in an old, long-established neighborhood.

■ IMPORTANT FEATURES THAT COUNT

Once homeseekers settle on an area they like, they tend to search for a house that contains specific features that they sorely miss in their present houses or apartments, according to a notable study, "What Makes the Home Buyer Tick?" by the late Pierre Martineau, who headed a market research group for the *Chicago Tribune.* The features sought may be a fully equipped modern kitchen, extra bedrooms, and plenty of storage and yard space, as well as insulation and a good heating system.

Some buyers, on the other hand, don't know exactly what they want until they are struck by certain features they see in houses that remind them of drastic shortcomings in their existing homes or apartments. Then their search for a house narrows down to one with special features that assume paramount importance to them. And once a couple recognizes the availability of new features and modern conveniences lacking in their present home, their dissatisfaction grows sharply, Martineau found. Their search for a house is spurred on in an "intensive frenzied" way.

This is also the time when a sales gimmick can hit them with great impact and exert enormous influence on the decision to buy a house, even though the feature is nothing special and even though the particular house is of no great distinction. Martineau pointed out that it may be a distinctive fireplace, a winding staircase, or a separate dining room. Sometimes it is merely a smart-looking metal covering on the heating furnace, giving the impression that it is an outstanding heating system. The buyer infers that the rest of the house must also be outstanding. That does it. Whether it is a gimmick or not, people already on the verge of buying, buy.

Actually these people have probably given much thought to the house. They may not have checked it with an educated eye, but no glaring flaws have come to their attention. They are emotionally set up. Almost any distinctive feature—or any gimmick—will at this very moment serve to trigger the purchase. The special feature they see at this moment is final confirmation that this is the house for them. They buy it.

■ THE MOMENT OF TRUTH

Is it really a good house? Is it one that the buyers will truly be satisfied with? Let's take stock of what researchers have found out about our homebuying motives. They can tell us about how to buy a house and, among other things, how to avoid the gimmick house. The time to take stock of your homebuying motives, of course, is before reaching that final stage when, being human, you find yourself caught up by momentum. You've looked at so many houses for so long that all you want to do is buy a house, almost any house, and get it over with.

A few things should be clear. What kind of house do you really want, and why? Get rid of preconceived ideas you may have about houses before you shop for a house. You may think you want only a new house or nothing but an old house. Whichever it is, you should have valid reasons for your choice. Some people simply want a house that will require a minimum of upkeep and maintenance and therefore justifiably want a new house. There's nothing wrong with that, but you should be reminded that some new houses come with drastic built-in defects. You should now know, however, about that kind of new house. Those who lean strongly toward an old house should accept one at its own terms, realizing that among other things the old-house lemon should certainly be avoided. You know now about that breed, too.

You need not be ruthlessly objective and totally unemotional about buying a house. Respect the idea that the purchase of a house should be done with a realistic, hardheaded attitude. Nonetheless, one of the best tests for buying a house is how you feel about the house. In fact, many a bad homebuying decision could have been averted had the buyers, husband and wife, paused before buying to probe their bedrock buying motives. What kind of a house do they really want? Where do they really want to live? And do they truly feel they have found a good house?

Also remember that there is no perfect house. It does not exist. But if you feel confident that you have found a good house at a good price, it is usually one that should cause you no regrets.

Buying a house is a fairly important thing in our lives. Its importance is summed up by Sir Winston Churchill's piercing comment that first "we shape our buildings and afterward our buildings shape us."

Buying and owning a really good, trouble-free house can be a never-ending source of great pleasure and satisfaction.

Checklist for Buying a House

■ ═══════════════════════════════ ■

Here is a review of the main points in this book to help you when you shop for a house and also to make a final check on a house that you are ready to buy. Remember, though, that practically no house will be perfect and that some of the best houses may be deficient here and there. That's to be expected. On the other hand, if a house scores low on numerous checklist items, you have fair warning that it is probably a bad house.

■ THE HIGH-PRICED HOUSE

☐ What is the fair market value of the house? Was this determined by a real estate appraiser? Is it comparable with the sales price?

☐ Does the house conform in price with comparable houses in the same area?

☐ Is the house located in a residential neighborhood that will retain its character and value, if not increase in desirability? Or is the neighborhood likely to deteriorate in value (and pull down the value of the house)?

☐ Have you had the house checked by a construction expert (even if it is a new house)?

☐ How much money will you have to spend for repairs and improvements if you buy it?

☐ How much is the house worth to you—the top price you are willing to pay?

☐ If you must sell the house in a year or two, will you be able to get back what you paid for it, or close to it? (This is a good check on whether you are paying too much.)

☐ If you are working with a real estate broker, does he or she represent you or the seller in the negotiation? If the agent is a subagent of the seller, be careful what you say.

☐ How long has the house been for sale? The longer it has been on the market, the more likely it can be bought at a reduced price.

☐ If you buy the house directly from the owner, will you get a break on the price (because the owner does not pay a real estate broker's commission)?

☐ Finally, is the house priced right, or is it overpriced? Answer this question quickly and objectively, and it's probably the right answer. If you hem and haw, trying to think of reasons why the house may be worth the price asked, then it's probably overpriced.

■ THE UNFORESEEN EXPENSES OF BUYING AND OWNING A HOUSE

☐ What are the total closing costs for the house? Can they be reduced? Have you compared them with closing costs at different banks?

☐ How much must you pay in advance for escrow real estate taxes?

☐ What are the total annual real estate taxes for the house?

☐ If you are buying a new house, how much money will you need for inevitable moving-in expenses (grass seed, landscaping, new appliances, curtains, window shades, etc.)?

☐ If you are buying an old house, how much money will be needed for repairs and modernization?

☐ Have you arranged for a low-cost homeowners insurance policy?

☐ Do you have enough cash to buy the house and also pay for all moving-in expenses?

☐ Are the real estate taxes likely to go up in the area? Putting it another way: Are new schools, new roads, sewers, and so on likely to be needed? Or are such services already there?

■ THE TIGHT MORTGAGE BIND

☐ Have you talked to different mortgage lenders to determine the best mortgage terms available? In other words, have you shopped around for the best mortgage deal?

☐ Have you considered a VA mortgage (if you are a veteran)? An FHA mortgage?

☐ Which is better for you, an adjustable-rate mortgage (ARM), or a fixed-rate mortgage? If interest rates are comparatively high when you buy a house and therefore likely to decline later, an ARM could be better. But you must be comfortable with it.

☐ Is a prepayment penalty fee stipulated in your mortgage? If possible, have it eliminated. It is becoming an unusual clause and will limit your future options.

☐ Can you afford the monthly payments required to repay the mortgage?

☐ Does the mortgage include small-print traps, such as an acceleration clause? If so, have them eliminated.

☐ Does it seem that the lender is charging an inordinate amount of junk fees? If there are any charges you don't understand, ask the lender for an explanation.

■ THE VANISHING BUILDER

☐ Have you checked on the credentials and past record of the builder?

❏ How long has the builder been established in business locally?

❏ Is the name of the builder's company, the firm you are legally buying the house from, the same name and same corporation he or she has used in the past?

❏ Have you talked with previous buyers of the builder's houses, asking them about their experiences with the builder?

❏ What kind of warranty do you get with the house?

❏ Does the builder really impress you as a well-established local builder who will be around in the future? Or is your suspicion stirred that the builder is not as reliable as you would like?

■ THE NO-DESIGN HOUSE

❏ Does the house have style and genuine good looks?

❏ Is the house a pure architectural style, all Colonial or any other traditional design? Or a true contemporary design?

❏ Does the house have good scale and proportion?

❏ Does the house have a good exposure, a good orientation in relation to the sun?

❏ Does the house take advantage of the best outdoor view?

❏ Is the house well located on its lot? Will you have privacy from the street and neighbors? Will the front area of the lot (the public zone) be easy to keep up and maintain? Will you have maximum use of your land on the sides of the house and in the back? Can you enter and leave the house quickly and conveniently?

■ THE GARBLED FLOOR PLAN

☐ Does the floor plan provide good circulation in and out of the house and from one room to another?

☐ Are the main zones of the house—living, working and sleeping—separated from each other?

☐ Do the number of floor levels—one or one-and-a-half stories, two stories, or split-level—offer the most advantages and greatest living convenience for your family?

☐ Is the interior of the house bright, cheerful and attractive?

☐ Does the kitchen have a central location?

☐ Is the kitchen well designed? Does it have an efficient work triangle, plenty of counterspace and storage, a good exposure and enough space for eating?

☐ Is the bathroom (or are the bathrooms) ample and well designed and properly located for convenient access and privacy?

☐ Other rooms: Are they large enough? Are they designed for adequate furniture placement?

☐ Are the windows large enough? Are they properly located to give ample light and a feeling of spaciousness without loss of privacy?

☐ Are the closets large enough? Is there plenty of storage for household items, linen and laundry as well as for clothing and personal possessions?

■ THE OLD-HOUSE LEMON

☐ Has the house been checked by a construction expert to determine if it is in structurally good condition?

☐ Does the price of the house compare favorably with the price of a comparable new house?

❏ How much money will it cost to repair, improve and, if necessary, modernize the house? Do you have fairly accurate estimates for such work?

❏ How much of a total dollar investment will the house require (sales price plus total estimated cost for improvements and repairs)? Will this total investment cause the house to be overimproved for its neighborhood?

❏ Do you feel that the house is in good condition and one that you really like and want?

■ THE MARGINAL HOUSE

❏ Does the construction of the house conform with FHA's Minimum Property Requirements, at the very least?

❏ Does the house rate high in quality features for the following important parts?

    ❏ Foundation walls

    ❏ Adequate termite safeguards

    ❏ Rugged, low-upkeep exterior walls and paint

    ❏ Tough interior wall surfaces

    ❏ Well-made, closely fitted flooring that will retain its appearance

    ❏ Top-quality national-brand windows and doors

    ❏ Kitchen countertops of a good plastic laminate (such as Formica), good kitchen cabinets, ample lighting and wiring outlets, and good ventilation

    ❏ Good-quality bathroom fixtures and accessories—that is, good lavatory, tub, toilet, faucets, shower nozzle, waterproof walls and floors

    ❏ Plumbing with ¾-to-1-inch supply from the street and copper or bronze piping

    ❏ Water heater that's large enough for your family and that carries a 10-year warranty

☐ Septic tank of 900 to 1,000 gallons capacity and adequate leaching field, based on a percolation test showing that the septic system will work in your ground

☐ Adequate electric wiring capacity: at least 240 volts and 100 amperes capacity, 15 to 20 wiring circuits, plus spare circuits for future electric appliances

☐ A good roofing material of adequate weight and seal-down roof shingles

☐ Door hardware of solid brass, solid bronze or solid aluminum, with a deadlock mechanism on exterior doors

■ THE ENERGY-GUZZLER HOUSE

☐ Are the walls, ceilings and, if necessary, the floor, adequately insulated? Does the insulation conform with minimum R-value standards?

☐ Is the house lined with a vapor barrier?

☐ In a new house is the heating system guaranteed to maintain the house at 70°F when the outdoor temperature is at its coldest locally? In other words, is the system large enough for the house in your region?

☐ Is the heating equipment of good, if not top, quality?

☐ Is the heating distribution system properly designed and installed—for example, perimeter ducts and exterior floor outlets with warm-air heat, plenty of baseboard radiation with hot-water heat, and medium- or low-density baseboards with electric heat?

☐ Does the heating system produce heat quickly and operate quietly? (Turn it on and see.)

☐ Is the fuel used, whether it's gas or oil, economical in your area? If electric heat is used, what is its estimated annual operating cost for the house?

❏ If the house is centrally air-conditioned, is the system capacity large enough for the house? The cooling system should be guaranteed to maintain the indoor air at no more than 75°F and 50 percent relative humidity when the outdoor heat is at its summer peak for your climate.

❏ Is the insulation adequate for air-conditioning?

❏ Are large window areas shaded from hot sunshine to keep down heat entry, hence keep down the cooling bills?

❏ If it is a new house without central air-conditioning, are provisions made for inexpensive installation of cooling later? Ducts and furnace blower should be large enough for cooling, a cooling-coil plenum should be installed in advance, and a spare electric circuit of adequate capacity should be installed for future air-conditioning.

■ THE GIMMICK HOUSE

❏ Does the house contain special eye-catching features that may seem to have special appeal but are not necessarily of special merit? In other words, are you attracted, unknowingly perhaps, by gimmick features?

❏ Do certain special features in the house tend to make you want to buy the house? Are they features that you can provide yourself in another, perhaps better, house at comparatively lower cost? Or are they intrinsic features that make it a really good house?

❏ What are the fundamental reasons why you (and your family) want a house and want the particular house you are considering?

❏ Have you thoroughly considered the kind of house you really want and need?

❏ Besides being of good design and construction, is the house one that you will really like and be satisfied with?

Index